DIVER'S LOG

BOOK

A BOSTON MILLS PRESS BOOK

Created by
Dean McConnachie and Christine Marks
ISBN-13: 978-1-55046-478-8
ISBN-10: 1-55046-478-7

Published by Boston Mills Press
132 Main Street, Erin, Ontario
Canada N0B 1T0
Tel 519-833-2407   Fax 519-833-2195
e-mail: books@bostonmillspress.com
www.bostonmillspress.com

In Canada:
Distributed by Firefly Books Ltd.
66 Leek Crescent, Richmond Hill
Ontario, Canada L4B 1H1

In the United States:
Distributed by Firefly Books (U.S.) Inc.
P.O. Box 1338, Ellicott Station
Buffalo, New York, USA 14205

The publisher gratefully acknowledges the financial support for our
publishing program by the Canada Council for the Arts, the Ontario Arts
Council and the Government of Canada through the Book Publishing
Industry Development Program.

Cover photograph by
Carlos Villoch/imagequestmarine.com

Back cover photograph and pages 9, 19 and 21 by
Jan Pisarczyk/Pirak Studios

Illustrations by Ron Milmine
Milmine Designs

Text and cover design by
Chris McCorkindale and Sue Breen
McCorkindale Advertising & Design

Printed in China

Personal Information

Name _____

Birthdate _____

Height _____

Weight _____

Eyes _____

Hair _____

Street _____

City _____

State/Province _____

Zip/Postal _____ Country _____

Home Phone _____ Business Phone _____

Cell _____ Fax _____

Email _____

Doctor _____ Phone _____

Blood Type _____ Medic Alert # _____

Allergies _____

DAN Member Number _____

Certified By _____ Number _____

In Case Of Emergency Notify

Name _____ Relationship _____

Phone _____

Name _____ Relationship _____

Phone _____

Diver Training Record

Course _____ Date _____

Instructor _____

Signature _____

Certification _____ Certification # _____

Comments _____

Course _____ Date _____

Instructor _____

Signature _____

Certification _____ Certification # _____

Comments _____

Course _____ Date _____

Instructor _____

Signature _____

Certification _____ Certification # _____

Comments _____

Course _____ Date _____

Instructor _____

Signature _____

Certification _____ Certification # _____

Comments _____

Diver Training Record

Course _____ Date _____

Instructor _____

Signature _____

Certification _____ Certification # _____

Comments _____

Course _____ Date _____

Instructor _____

Signature _____

Certification _____ Certification # _____

Comments _____

Course _____ Date _____

Instructor _____

Signature _____

Certification _____ Certification # _____

Comments _____

Course _____ Date _____

Instructor _____

Signature _____

Certification _____ Certification # _____

Comments _____

Hand Signals

(Are you) OK!

OK? or OK! (On Surface)

OK? or OK! (One Arm Occupied)

HELP! EMERGENCY

TROUBLE
(Point to the area of trouble and shake head NO)

ASSEMBLE HERE

THIS LEVEL

OUT OF AIR

LOW ON AIR

I AM COLD

(I'm feeling the effects of) NARCOSIS

LOOK! DANGER
(Shake head NO)

ASCEND

DESCEND

BOAT

Hand Signals

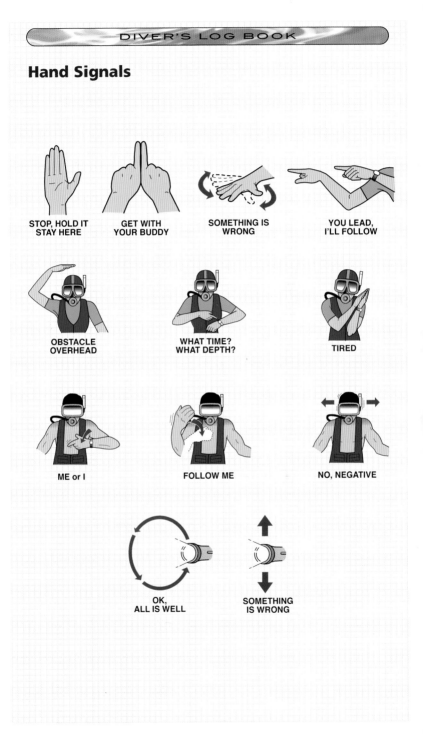

STOP, HOLD IT
STAY HERE

GET WITH
YOUR BUDDY

SOMETHING IS
WRONG

YOU LEAD,
I'LL FOLLOW

OBSTACLE
OVERHEAD

WHAT TIME?
WHAT DEPTH?

TIRED

ME or I

FOLLOW ME

NO, NEGATIVE

OK,
ALL IS WELL

SOMETHING
IS WRONG

The Dive Flag

The dive flag is used by divers to signal to boat operators that there is a diver below and to stay clear. The flag should be raised and flown while divers are in the water. Boaters are required to stay clear of any vessel showing a Dive Flag. The distance of clearance varies from state to state, province to province, and country to country. In general the clearance is expected to be between 100 and 150 feet (30 to 50 meters).

To this day, many boat operators are still not aware of the meaning of this flag. This is NOT a legal mandate but is based on cooperation, therefore it is very important that divers take as many precautions as possible to avoid injury.

Diver Down Flag
- White Diagonal on Red Flag
- North American Recognition

Alpha Flag
- Blue and White
- International

Diver Recall Flag
Return to vessel immediately
- White Rectangle on Red Flag
- International

CHECKLISTS AND RECORDS

Diving Equipment Checklist

- Swimsuit
- Mask
- Anti-fog spray
- Snorkel & keeper
- Fins
- Wetsuit—Drysuit
  - Jacket
  - Farmer John
  - Boots
  - Hood
  - Gloves
  - Liner
- Weight belt
- Ankle weights
- Buoyancy compensator
- Full tank
- Full pony bottle
- Regulator
- Dive watch
- Computer
- Compass
- Underwater tables
- Whistle
- Light
- Knife
- Float N Flag
- Gear bag
- Wreck reel
- Safety line
- Safety sausage
- Lift bag
- Slate and pencil
- Extra weight

Other Equipment Checklist

- Video camera
- Still camera
- Camera batteries
- Film / tape
- Strobe
- Video lights
- Light batteries
- Battery chargers
- Dry sack
- Silicon lube
- Spear gun
- _____
- _____
- _____
- _____
- _____
- _____

- _____
- _____
- _____
- _____
- _____
- _____

Emergency Repair Kit

- Mask strap
- Fin strap
- O rings
- Reg. high-pressure plug
- Silicon lube
- Wetsuit cement
- Needle thread
- Waterproof tape
- Waterproof bag
- BC bladder patches
- _____
- _____
- _____
- _____

Other Items Checklist

- Dry clothes
- Towel
- Food
- Drinking water
- Sunglasses
- Sunscreen
- Log book
- Pen and pencil
- Credit cards
- Maps
- GPS
- Cell phone
- Marine radio
- Passport
- Additional travel insurance
- _____
- _____

First Aid Kit

- Adhesive tape
- Alcohol solution (70%)
- Ammonia solution
- Antiseptic spray
- Butterfly strips
- Band aids
- Compresses
- Cotton swabs
- Razor blade / knife
- Scissors
- Snakebite kit
- Sea-sickness pills
- Soap
- Splints
- Nasal decongestant
- Ear drops
- Baking soda
- Vinegar
- Sunburn cream
- Tylenol / aspirin
- DAN 02 kit
- _____
- _____
- _____
- _____
- _____
- _____
- _____
- _____
- _____
- _____

Equipment Record

Mask 1 Manufacturer _____ Model _____

Date Purchased _____ From _____

Size _____ Color _____

Mask 2 Manufacturer _____ Model _____

Date Purchased _____ From _____

Size _____ Color _____

Snorkel Manufacturer _____ Model _____

Date Purchased _____ From _____

Size _____ Color _____

Fins Manufacturer _____ Model _____

Date Purchased _____ From _____

Size _____ Color _____

Weight Belt ● Hard Weights ● Soft Weights

Date Purchased _____ From _____

Weight _____ Color _____

Dive Knife Manufacturer _____ Model _____

Date Purchased _____ From _____

Size _____ Color _____

Dive Light Manufacturer _____ Model _____

Date Purchased _____ From _____

Size _____ Color _____

Compass Manufacturer _____ Model _____

Date Purchased _____ From _____

Size _____ Color _____

Equipment Record

Wetsuit Manufacturer _____

Date Purchased _____ From _____

Jacket Size _____ Body Size _____

Hood Size _____ Glove Size _____

Boot Size _____ Color _____

Drysuit Manufacturer _____

Date Purchased _____ From _____

Liner Size _____ Body Size _____

Hood Size _____ Glove Size _____

Boot Size _____ Color _____

Regulator Manufacturer _____ Model _____

Date Purchased _____ From _____

First Stage S/N _____

Second Stage S/N _____

Octopus S/N _____

Regulator Manufacturer _____ Model _____

Date Purchased _____ From _____

First Stage S/N _____

Second Stage S/N _____

Octopus S/N _____

Dive Computer Manufacturer _____ Model _____

Date Purchased _____ From _____

S/N Color _____

BC Manufacturer _____ Model _____

Date Purchased _____ From _____

Size _____ Color _____

Equipment Maintenance Record

Regulator Model _____

S/N _____

Service Date _____ Service By _____

Comments _____

_____

Regulator Model _____

S/N _____

Service Date _____ Service By _____

Comments _____

_____

Regulator Model _____

S/N _____

Service Date _____ Service By _____

Comments _____

_____

Regulator Model _____

S/N _____

Service Date _____ Service By _____

Comments _____

_____

Equipment Maintenance Record

Regulator Model _____

S/N _____

Service Date _____ Service By _____

Comments _____

_____

Regulator Model _____

S/N _____

Service Date _____ Service By _____

Comments _____

_____

Regulator Model _____

S/N _____

Service Date _____ Service By _____

Comments _____

_____

Regulator Model _____

S/N _____

Service Date _____ Service By _____

Comments _____

_____

Equipment Maintenance Record

Tank Manufacturer _____

Date Purchased _____ From _____

Size: _____ ⚪ Steel ⚪ Aluminium

Color _____ S/N _____

Initial Hydro Date _____ Initial Visual Date _____

Service Date _____ Visual Hydro Nitrox Clean

Service Date _____ Visual Hydro Nitrox Clean

Service Date _____ Visual Hydro Nitrox Clean

Service Date _____ Visual Hydro Nitrox Clean

Service Date _____ Visual Hydro Nitrox Clean

Service Date _____ Visual Hydro Nitrox Clean

Tank Manufacturer _____

Date Purchased _____ From _____

Size: _____ ⚪ Steel ⚪ Aluminium

Color _____ S/N _____

Initial Hydro Date _____ Initial Visual Date _____

Service Date _____ Visual Hydro Nitrox Clean

Service Date _____ Visual Hydro Nitrox Clean

Service Date _____ Visual Hydro Nitrox Clean

Service Date _____ Visual Hydro Nitrox Clean

Service Date _____ Visual Hydro Nitrox Clean

Service Date _____ Visual Hydro Nitrox Clean

Equipment Maintenance Record

Tank Manufacturer _____

Date Purchased _____ From _____

Size: _____ ● Steel ● Aluminium

Color _____ S/N _____

Initial Hydro Date _____ Initial Visual Date _____

Service Date _____ Visual Hydro Nitrox Clean

Service Date _____ Visual Hydro Nitrox Clean

Service Date _____ Visual Hydro Nitrox Clean

Service Date _____ Visual Hydro Nitrox Clean

Service Date _____ Visual Hydro Nitrox Clean

Service Date _____ Visual Hydro Nitrox Clean

Tank Manufacturer _____

Date Purchased _____ From _____

Size: _____ ● Steel ● Aluminium

Color _____ S/N _____

Initial Hydro Date _____ Initial Visual Date _____

Service Date _____ Visual Hydro Nitrox Clean

Service Date _____ Visual Hydro Nitrox Clean

Service Date _____ Visual Hydro Nitrox Clean

Service Date _____ Visual Hydro Nitrox Clean

Service Date _____ Visual Hydro Nitrox Clean

Service Date _____ Visual Hydro Nitrox Clean

Equipment Maintenance Record

Tank Manufacturer _____

Date Purchased _____ From _____

Size: _____ ⚪ Steel ⚪ Aluminium

Color _____ S/N _____

Initial Hydro Date _____ Initial Visual Date _____

Service Date _____ Visual Hydro Nitrox Clean

Service Date _____ Visual Hydro Nitrox Clean

Service Date _____ Visual Hydro Nitrox Clean

Service Date _____ Visual Hydro Nitrox Clean

Service Date _____ Visual Hydro Nitrox Clean

Service Date _____ Visual Hydro Nitrox Clean

Tank Manufacturer _____

Date Purchased _____ From _____

Size: _____ ⚪ Steel ⚪ Aluminium

Color _____ S/N _____

Initial Hydro Date _____ Initial Visual Date _____

Service Date _____ Visual Hydro Nitrox Clean

Service Date _____ Visual Hydro Nitrox Clean

Service Date _____ Visual Hydro Nitrox Clean

Service Date _____ Visual Hydro Nitrox Clean

Service Date _____ Visual Hydro Nitrox Clean

Service Date _____ Visual Hydro Nitrox Clean

DIVES

DIVER'S LOG BOOK

Dive Number: 453	Date: March 22, 2005
Location: Curacao, Lesser Antilles	
GPS: N78°85'125 W78°54'125	
Body of Water: South Shore	
Site: Mushroom Forest	

Dive Class

- ● Wreck
- ● Boat
- ● Shore
- ● Certify
- ● Reef
- ● Photo
- ● River
- ● Video
- ● Ice
- ● _____
- ● Deep
- ● _____
- ● Cave
- ● _____

Weather	☾	❄	🌧	⛅	☀
Air Temp C/F	-10/14	0/32	10/50	20/68	30/86	40/104
Surface Temp	-10/14	0/32	10/50	20/68	30/86	40/104
Temp @ Depth	-10/14	0/32	10/50	20/68	30/86	40/104
Surface	Calm		Choppy		Waves
Current	None				Swift
Visibility M/ft	0	7.5/25	15/50	23/75	30/100

Dive Profile

● First Dive　● Second Dive　● Third Dive

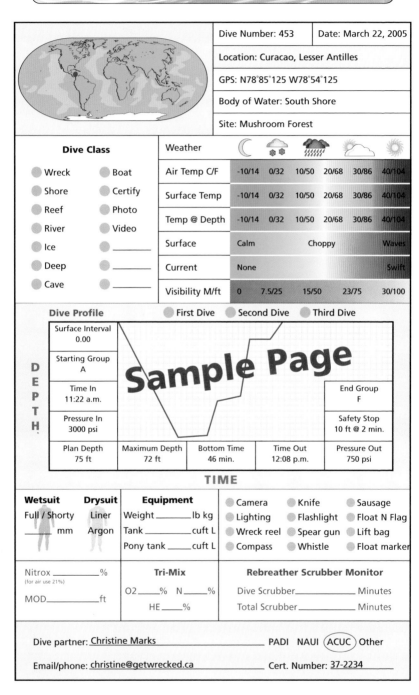

DEPTH

Surface Interval 0.00				
Starting Group A				
Time In 11:22 a.m.			End Group F	
Pressure In 3000 psi			Safety Stop 10 ft @ 2 min.	
Plan Depth 75 ft	Maximum Depth 72 ft	Bottom Time 46 min.	Time Out 12:08 p.m.	Pressure Out 750 psi

Sample Page

TIME

Wetsuit	**Drysuit**	**Equipment**			
Full / Shorty	Liner	Weight _____ lb kg	● Camera	● Knife	● Sausage
_____ mm	Argon	Tank _____ cuft L	● Lighting	● Flashlight	● Float N Flag
		Pony tank _____ cuft L	● Wreck reel	● Spear gun	● Lift bag
			● Compass	● Whistle	● Float marker

Nitrox _____% (for air use 21%) MOD _____ ft	**Tri-Mix** O2 ____% N ____% HE ____%	**Rebreather Scrubber Monitor** Dive Scrubber _____ Minutes Total Scrubber _____ Minutes

Dive partner: <u>Christine Marks</u>　　　　PADI　NAUI　(ACUC)　Other

Email/phone: <u>christine@getwrecked.ca</u>　　　　Cert. Number: <u>37-2234</u>

Sightings, Hazards, Notes, Photos, Sketches

Spotted a parrotfish, a pod of squid, Eagle Rays (wow) and a lot of Sea Turtles. The turtles didn't seem very interested in us.

Wicked dive anytime I am here. Always on the lookout for Frog Fish and Sea Horses but no luck today. Ah well.

Weather is amazing. Tito the dive master has looked after Chris. She has been spoiled rotten for her first "southern trip."

Sample Page

	Dive Number:	Date:
	Location:	
	GPS:	
	Body of Water:	
	Site:	

Dive Class

- Wreck
- Shore
- Reef
- River
- Ice
- Deep
- Cave

- Boat
- Certify
- Photo
- Video
- _____
- _____
- _____

Weather	☾	❄	🌧	⛅	☀
Air Temp C/F	-10/14	0/32	10/50	20/68	30/86	40/104
Surface Temp	-10/14	0/32	10/50	20/68	30/86	40/104
Temp @ Depth	-10/14	0/32	10/50	20/68	30/86	40/104
Surface	Calm		Choppy		Waves
Current	None				Swift
Visibility M/ft	0	7.5/25	15/50	23/75	30/100

Dive Profile

○ First Dive   ○ Second Dive   ○ Third Dive

DEPTH

Surface Interval	
Starting Group	
Time In	End Group
Pressure In	Safety Stop

Plan Depth	Maximum Depth	Bottom Time	Time Out	Pressure Out

TIME

Wetsuit **Drysuit**

Full / Shorty   Liner

_____ mm   Argon

Equipment

Weight _____ lb kg

Tank _____ cuft L

Pony tank _____ cuft L

- Camera
- Lighting
- Wreck reel
- Compass

- Knife
- Flashlight
- Spear gun
- Whistle

- Sausage
- Float N Flag
- Lift bag
- Float marker

Nitrox _____ %
(for air use 21%)

MOD _____ ft

Tri-Mix

O2 _____ % N _____ %

HE _____ %

Rebreather Scrubber Monitor

Dive Scrubber _____ Minutes

Total Scrubber _____ Minutes

Dive partner: _____ PADI NAUI ACUC Other

Email/phone: _____ Cert. Number: _____

Sightings, Hazards, Notes, Photos, Sketches

DIVER'S LOG BOOK

	Dive Number:	Date:
	Location:	
	GPS:	
	Body of Water:	
	Site:	

Dive Class

- Wreck
- Boat
- Shore
- Certify
- Reef
- Photo
- River
- Video
- Ice
- _____
- Deep
- _____
- Cave
- _____

Weather	☾	☁❄	🌧	⛅	☀
Air Temp C/F	-10/14	0/32	10/50	20/68	30/86	40/104
Surface Temp	-10/14	0/32	10/50	20/68	30/86	40/104
Temp @ Depth	-10/14	0/32	10/50	20/68	30/86	40/104
Surface	Calm		Choppy		Waves
Current	None				Swift
Visibility M/ft	0	7.5/25	15/50	23/75	30/100

Dive Profile

- First Dive
- Second Dive
- Third Dive

D E P T H

Surface Interval				
Starting Group				
Time In				End Group
Pressure In				Safety Stop
Plan Depth	Maximum Depth	Bottom Time	Time Out	Pressure Out

TIME

Wetsuit
Full / Shorty
_____ mm

Drysuit
Liner
Argon

Equipment
Weight _____ lb kg
Tank _____ cuft L
Pony tank _____ cuft L

- Camera
- Knife
- Sausage
- Lighting
- Flashlight
- Float N Flag
- Wreck reel
- Spear gun
- Lift bag
- Compass
- Whistle
- Float marker

Nitrox _____ %
(for air use 21%)

MOD_____ ft

Tri-Mix
O2 ____ % N ____ %
HE ____ %

Rebreather Scrubber Monitor
Dive Scrubber_____ Minutes
Total Scrubber_____ Minutes

Dive partner:_____ PADI NAUI ACUC Other

Email/phone: _____ Cert. Number: _____

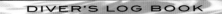

Sightings, Hazards, Notes, Photos, Sketches

DIVER'S LOG BOOK

Dive Number:	Date:
Location:	
GPS:	
Body of Water:	
Site:	

Dive Class

- Wreck
- Shore
- Reef
- River
- Ice
- Deep
- Cave
- Boat
- Certify
- Photo
- Video
- _____
- _____
- _____

Weather	☾	❄	☔	⛅	☀
Air Temp C/F	-10/14	0/32	10/50	20/68	30/86	40/104
Surface Temp	-10/14	0/32	10/50	20/68	30/86	40/104
Temp @ Depth	-10/14	0/32	10/50	20/68	30/86	40/104
Surface	Calm		Choppy		Waves
Current	None				Swift
Visibility M/ft	0	7.5/25	15/50	23/75	30/100

Dive Profile

- First Dive
- Second Dive
- Third Dive

DEPTH

Surface Interval	
Starting Group	
Time In	End Group
Pressure In	Safety Stop

Plan Depth	Maximum Depth	Bottom Time	Time Out	Pressure Out

TIME

Wetsuit	**Drysuit**	**Equipment**
Full / Shorty	Liner	Weight _____ lb kg
_____ mm	Argon	Tank _____ cuft L
		Pony tank _____ cuft L

- Camera
- Lighting
- Wreck reel
- Compass
- Knife
- Flashlight
- Spear gun
- Whistle
- Sausage
- Float N Flag
- Lift bag
- Float marker

Nitrox _____ %
(for air use 21%)

MOD _____ ft

Tri-Mix

O2 _____ % N _____ %

HE _____ %

Rebreather Scrubber Monitor

Dive Scrubber _____ Minutes

Total Scrubber _____ Minutes

Dive partner: _____ PADI NAUI ACUC Other

Email/phone: _____ Cert. Number: _____

DIVER'S LOG BOOK

Sightings, Hazards, Notes, Photos, Sketches

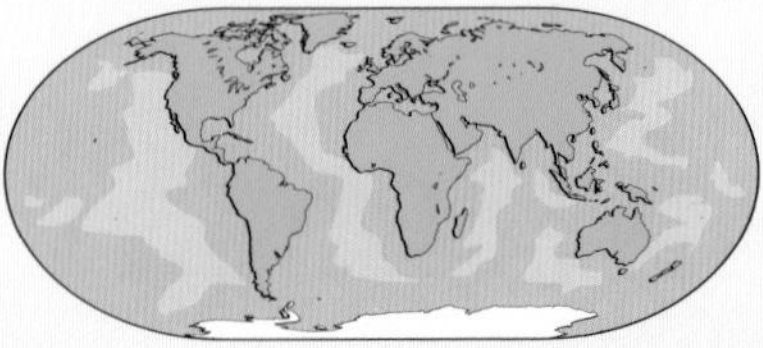

DIVER'S LOG BOOK

Dive Number:		Date:
Location:		
GPS:		
Body of Water:		
Site:		

Dive Class

- Wreck
- Shore
- Reef
- River
- Ice
- Deep
- Cave
- Boat
- Certify
- Photo
- Video
- _____
- _____
- _____

Weather	☾	❄	☔	☁	☀
Air Temp C/F	-10/14	0/32	10/50	20/68	30/86	40/104
Surface Temp	-10/14	0/32	10/50	20/68	30/86	40/104
Temp @ Depth	-10/14	0/32	10/50	20/68	30/86	40/104
Surface	Calm		Choppy		Waves
Current	None				Swift
Visibility M/ft	0	7.5/25	15/50	23/75	30/100

Dive Profile

- First Dive
- Second Dive
- Third Dive

Surface Interval				
Starting Group				
Time In				End Group
Pressure In				Safety Stop
Plan Depth	Maximum Depth	Bottom Time	Time Out	Pressure Out

DEPTH (vertical, left axis)

TIME

Wetsuit	**Drysuit**	**Equipment**
Full / Shorty	Liner	Weight _____ lb kg
_____ mm	Argon	Tank _____ cuft L
		Pony tank _____ cuft L

- Camera
- Lighting
- Wreck reel
- Compass
- Knife
- Flashlight
- Spear gun
- Whistle
- Sausage
- Float N Flag
- Lift bag
- Float marker

Nitrox _____% (for air use 21%) MOD_____ft	**Tri-Mix** O2 _____% N _____% HE _____%	**Rebreather Scrubber Monitor** Dive Scrubber_____ Minutes Total Scrubber _____ Minutes

Dive partner:_____ PADI NAUI ACUC Other

Email/phone:_____ Cert. Number: _____

Sightings, Hazards, Notes, Photos, Sketches

	Dive Number:	Date:
	Location:	
	GPS:	
	Body of Water:	
	Site:	

Dive Class

- Wreck
- Shore
- Reef
- River
- Ice
- Deep
- Cave
- Boat
- Certify
- Photo
- Video
- _____
- _____
- _____

Weather	☾	☁❄	🌧	⛅	☀
Air Temp C/F	-10/14	0/32	10/50	20/68	30/86	40/104
Surface Temp	-10/14	0/32	10/50	20/68	30/86	40/104
Temp @ Depth	-10/14	0/32	10/50	20/68	30/86	40/104
Surface	Calm		Choppy		Waves
Current	None				Swift
Visibility M/ft	0	7.5/25	15/50	23/75	30/100

Dive Profile

○ First Dive   ○ Second Dive   ○ Third Dive

DEPTH

Surface Interval				
Starting Group				
Time In				End Group
Pressure In				Safety Stop
Plan Depth	Maximum Depth	Bottom Time	Time Out	Pressure Out

TIME

Wetsuit **Drysuit**
Full / Shorty Liner
_____ mm Argon

Equipment
Weight _____ lb kg
Tank _____ cuft L
Pony tank _____ cuft L

- Camera
- Lighting
- Wreck reel
- Compass
- Knife
- Flashlight
- Spear gun
- Whistle
- Sausage
- Float N Flag
- Lift bag
- Float marker

Nitrox _____ %
(for air use 21%)
MOD _____ ft

Tri-Mix
O2 _____ % N _____ %
HE _____ %

Rebreather Scrubber Monitor
Dive Scrubber _____ Minutes
Total Scrubber _____ Minutes

Dive partner: _____ PADI NAUI ACUC Other

Email/phone: _____ Cert. Number: _____

Sightings, Hazards, Notes, Photos, Sketches

DIVER'S LOG BOOK

Dive Number:	Date:

Location:
GPS:
Body of Water:
Site:

Dive Class

- Wreck
- Shore
- Reef
- River
- Ice
- Deep
- Cave
- Boat
- Certify
- Photo
- Video
- _____
- _____
- _____

Weather	☾	❄	🌧	⛅	☀
Air Temp C/F	-10/14	0/32	10/50	20/68	30/86	40/104
Surface Temp	-10/14	0/32	10/50	20/68	30/86	40/104
Temp @ Depth	-10/14	0/32	10/50	20/68	30/86	40/104
Surface	Calm		Choppy		Waves
Current	None				Swift
Visibility M/ft	0	7.5/25	15/50	23/75	30/100

Dive Profile

- First Dive
- Second Dive
- Third Dive

DEPTH

Surface Interval				
Starting Group				
Time In				End Group
Pressure In				Safety Stop
Plan Depth	Maximum Depth	Bottom Time	Time Out	Pressure Out

TIME

Wetsuit	**Drysuit**
Full / Shorty	Liner
____ mm	Argon

Equipment

Weight _____ lb kg
Tank _____ cuft L
Pony tank _____ cuft L

- Camera
- Lighting
- Wreck reel
- Compass
- Knife
- Flashlight
- Spear gun
- Whistle
- Sausage
- Float N Flag
- Lift bag
- Float marker

Nitrox _____%
(for air use 21%)

MOD_____ft

Tri-Mix

O2 ____% N ____%
HE ____%

Rebreather Scrubber Monitor

Dive Scrubber_____ Minutes
Total Scrubber _____ Minutes

Dive partner:_____ PADI NAUI ACUC Other

Email/phone: _____ Cert. Number: _____

Sightings, Hazards, Notes, Photos, Sketches

Dive Number:	Date:
Location:	
GPS:	
Body of Water:	
Site:	

Dive Class

- Wreck
- Shore
- Reef
- River
- Ice
- Deep
- Cave

- Boat
- Certify
- Photo
- Video
- _____
- _____
- _____

Weather	🌙	☁️❄️	🌧️	☁️	☀️
Air Temp C/F	-10/14	0/32	10/50	20/68	30/86	40/104
Surface Temp	-10/14	0/32	10/50	20/68	30/86	40/104
Temp @ Depth	-10/14	0/32	10/50	20/68	30/86	40/104
Surface	Calm		Choppy		Waves
Current	None				Swift
Visibility M/ft	0	7.5/25	15/50	23/75	30/100

Dive Profile

- First Dive
- Second Dive
- Third Dive

DEPTH

Surface Interval		
Starting Group		
Time In		End Group
Pressure In		Safety Stop

Plan Depth	Maximum Depth	Bottom Time	Time Out	Pressure Out

TIME

Wetsuit	**Drysuit**	**Equipment**		
Full / Shorty	Liner	Weight _____ lb kg		
_____ mm	Argon	Tank _____ cuft L		
		Pony tank _____ cuft L		

- Camera
- Lighting
- Wreck reel
- Compass

- Knife
- Flashlight
- Spear gun
- Whistle

- Sausage
- Float N Flag
- Lift bag
- Float marker

Nitrox _____ %
(for air use 21%)

MOD _____ ft

Tri-Mix

O2 _____ % N _____ %

HE _____ %

Rebreather Scrubber Monitor

Dive Scrubber _____ Minutes

Total Scrubber _____ Minutes

Dive partner: _____ PADI NAUI ACUC Other

Email/phone: _____ Cert. Number: _____

DIVER'S LOG BOOK

Sightings, Hazards, Notes, Photos, Sketches

	Dive Number:	Date:
	Location:	
	GPS:	
	Body of Water:	
	Site:	

Dive Class

- Wreck
- Shore
- Reef
- River
- Ice
- Deep
- Cave

- Boat
- Certify
- Photo
- Video
- _____
- _____
- _____

Weather	☾	❄	🌧	☁	☀
Air Temp C/F	-10/14	0/32	10/50	20/68	30/86	40/104
Surface Temp	-10/14	0/32	10/50	20/68	30/86	40/104
Temp @ Depth	-10/14	0/32	10/50	20/68	30/86	40/104
Surface	Calm		Choppy		Waves
Current	None				Swift
Visibility M/ft	0	7.5/25	15/50	23/75	30/100

Dive Profile

- First Dive
- Second Dive
- Third Dive

D E P T H

Surface Interval				
Starting Group				
Time In			End Group	
Pressure In			Safety Stop	
Plan Depth	Maximum Depth	Bottom Time	Time Out	Pressure Out

TIME

Wetsuit	**Drysuit**	**Equipment**	
Full / Shorty	Liner	Weight _____lb kg	
_____ mm	Argon	Tank _____cuft L	
		Pony tank _____cuft L	

- Camera
- Lighting
- Wreck reel
- Compass

- Knife
- Flashlight
- Spear gun
- Whistle

- Sausage
- Float N Flag
- Lift bag
- Float marker

Nitrox _____% (for air use 21%)	**Tri-Mix**	**Rebreather Scrubber Monitor**
MOD_____ft	O2 ____% N ____%	Dive Scrubber_____ Minutes
	HE ____%	Total Scrubber_____ Minutes

Dive partner:_____ PADI NAUI ACUC Other

Email/phone:_____ Cert. Number: _____

DIVER'S LOG BOOK

Sightings, Hazards, Notes, Photos, Sketches

Dive Number:	Date:
Location:	
GPS:	
Body of Water:	
Site:	

Dive Class

- Wreck
- Shore
- Reef
- River
- Ice
- Deep
- Cave
- Boat
- Certify
- Photo
- Video
- _____
- _____
- _____

Weather	🌙	❄️	🌧️	⛅	☀️
Air Temp C/F	-10/14	0/32	10/50	20/68	30/86	40/104
Surface Temp	-10/14	0/32	10/50	20/68	30/86	40/104
Temp @ Depth	-10/14	0/32	10/50	20/68	30/86	40/104
Surface	Calm		Choppy		Waves
Current	None				Swift
Visibility M/ft	0	7.5/25	15/50	23/75	30/100

Dive Profile

- First Dive
- Second Dive
- Third Dive

D E P T H

Surface Interval		
Starting Group		
Time In		End Group
Pressure In		Safety Stop

Plan Depth	Maximum Depth	Bottom Time	Time Out	Pressure Out

TIME

Wetsuit
Full / Shorty
_____ mm

Drysuit
Liner
Argon

Equipment
Weight _____ lb kg
Tank _____ cuft L
Pony tank _____ cuft L

- Camera
- Lighting
- Wreck reel
- Compass
- Knife
- Flashlight
- Spear gun
- Whistle
- Sausage
- Float N Flag
- Lift bag
- Float marker

Nitrox _____ %
(for air use 21%)

MOD _____ ft

Tri-Mix
O2 _____ % N _____ %
HE _____ %

Rebreather Scrubber Monitor
Dive Scrubber _____ Minutes
Total Scrubber _____ Minutes

Dive partner: _____ PADI NAUI ACUC Other

Email/phone: _____ Cert. Number: _____

DIVER'S LOG BOOK

Sightings, Hazards, Notes, Photos, Sketches

DIVER'S LOG BOOK

Dive Number:		Date:
Location:		
GPS:		
Body of Water:		
Site:		

Dive Class

- Wreck
- Boat
- Shore
- Certify
- Reef
- Photo
- River
- Video
- Ice
- _____
- Deep
- _____
- Cave
- _____

Weather					
Air Temp C/F	-10/14	0/32	10/50	20/68	30/86	40/104
Surface Temp	-10/14	0/32	10/50	20/68	30/86	40/104
Temp @ Depth	-10/14	0/32	10/50	20/68	30/86	40/104
Surface	Calm		Choppy			Waves
Current	None					Swift
Visibility M/ft	0	7.5/25	15/50	23/75	30/100

Dive Profile

- First Dive
- Second Dive
- Third Dive

DEPTH

Surface Interval				
Starting Group				
Time In				End Group
Pressure In				Safety Stop
Plan Depth	Maximum Depth	Bottom Time	Time Out	Pressure Out

TIME

Wetsuit	**Drysuit**	**Equipment**		
Full / Shorty	Liner	Weight _____ lb kg		
_____ mm	Argon	Tank _____ cuft L		
		Pony tank _____ cuft L		

- Camera
- Knife
- Sausage
- Lighting
- Flashlight
- Float N Flag
- Wreck reel
- Spear gun
- Lift bag
- Compass
- Whistle
- Float marker

Nitrox _____ %
(for air use 21%)

MOD _____ ft

Tri-Mix

O2 _____ % N _____ %

HE _____ %

Rebreather Scrubber Monitor

Dive Scrubber _____ Minutes

Total Scrubber _____ Minutes

Dive partner: _____ PADI NAUI ACUC Other

Email/phone: _____ Cert. Number: _____

Sightings, Hazards, Notes, Photos, Sketches

DIVER'S LOG BOOK

Dive Number:		Date:	
Location:			
GPS:			
Body of Water:			
Site:			

Dive Class

- Wreck
- Shore
- Reef
- River
- Ice
- Deep
- Cave
- Boat
- Certify
- Photo
- Video
- _____
- _____
- _____

Weather	☾	❄	🌧	⛅	☀
Air Temp C/F	-10/14	0/32	10/50	20/68	30/86	40/104
Surface Temp	-10/14	0/32	10/50	20/68	30/86	40/104
Temp @ Depth	-10/14	0/32	10/50	20/68	30/86	40/104
Surface	Calm		Choppy		Waves
Current	None				Swift
Visibility M/ft	0	7.5/25	15/50	23/75	30/100

Dive Profile
- First Dive
- Second Dive
- Third Dive

DEPTH

Surface Interval			
Starting Group			
Time In			End Group
Pressure In			Safety Stop
Plan Depth	Maximum Depth	Bottom Time	Time Out	Pressure Out

TIME

Wetsuit	Drysuit	Equipment		
Full / Shorty	Liner	Weight _____ lb kg		
_____ mm	Argon	Tank _____ cuft L		
		Pony tank _____ cuft L		

- Camera
- Lighting
- Wreck reel
- Compass
- Knife
- Flashlight
- Spear gun
- Whistle
- Sausage
- Float N Flag
- Lift bag
- Float marker

Nitrox _____ %
(for air use 21%)

MOD _____ ft

Tri-Mix

O2 _____ % N _____ %

HE _____ %

Rebreather Scrubber Monitor

Dive Scrubber _____ Minutes

Total Scrubber _____ Minutes

Dive partner: _____ PADI NAUI ACUC Other

Email/phone: _____ Cert. Number: _____

Sightings, Hazards, Notes, Photos, Sketches

Dive Number:	Date:

Location:
GPS:
Body of Water:
Site:

Dive Class

- Wreck
- Shore
- Reef
- River
- Ice
- Deep
- Cave
- Boat
- Certify
- Photo
- Video
- _____
- _____
- _____

Weather	🌙	❄️	🌧️	☁️	☀️
Air Temp C/F	-10/14	0/32	10/50	20/68	30/86	40/104
Surface Temp	-10/14	0/32	10/50	20/68	30/86	40/104
Temp @ Depth	-10/14	0/32	10/50	20/68	30/86	40/104
Surface	Calm		Choppy		Waves
Current	None				Swift
Visibility M/ft	0	7.5/25	15/50	23/75	30/100

Dive Profile

- First Dive
- Second Dive
- Third Dive

D E P T H	Surface Interval			
	Starting Group			
	Time In			End Group
	Pressure In			Safety Stop
	Plan Depth	Maximum Depth	Bottom Time	Time Out	Pressure Out

TIME

Wetsuit	**Drysuit**
Full / Shorty	Liner
_____ mm	Argon

Equipment

Weight _____ lb kg
Tank _____ cuft L
Pony tank _____ cuft L

- Camera
- Lighting
- Wreck reel
- Compass
- Knife
- Flashlight
- Spear gun
- Whistle
- Sausage
- Float N Flag
- Lift bag
- Float marker

Nitrox _____ %
(for air use 21%)

MOD_____ ft

Tri-Mix

O2 _____ % N _____ %
HE _____ %

Rebreather Scrubber Monitor

Dive Scrubber_____ Minutes
Total Scrubber_____ Minutes

Dive partner:_____ PADI NAUI ACUC Other

Email/phone:_____ Cert. Number: _____

Sightings, Hazards, Notes, Photos, Sketches

DIVER'S LOG BOOK

Dive Number:	Date:
Location:	
GPS:	
Body of Water:	
Site:	

Dive Class

- Wreck
- Shore
- Reef
- River
- Ice
- Deep
- Cave
- Boat
- Certify
- Photo
- Video
- _____
- _____
- _____

Weather	🌙	🌨	🌧	⛅	☀
Air Temp C/F	-10/14	0/32	10/50	20/68	30/86	40/104
Surface Temp	-10/14	0/32	10/50	20/68	30/86	40/104
Temp @ Depth	-10/14	0/32	10/50	20/68	30/86	40/104
Surface	Calm		Choppy		Waves
Current	None				Swift
Visibility M/ft	0	7.5/25	15/50	23/75	30/100

Dive Profile

- First Dive
- Second Dive
- Third Dive

DEPTH

Surface Interval				
Starting Group				
Time In			End Group	
Pressure In			Safety Stop	
Plan Depth	Maximum Depth	Bottom Time	Time Out	Pressure Out

TIME

Wetsuit	**Drysuit**	**Equipment**
Full / Shorty	Liner	Weight _____ lb kg
_____ mm	Argon	Tank _____ cuft L
		Pony tank _____ cuft L

- Camera
- Lighting
- Wreck reel
- Compass
- Knife
- Flashlight
- Spear gun
- Whistle
- Sausage
- Float N Flag
- Lift bag
- Float marker

Nitrox _____%
(for air use 21%)

MOD_____ft

Tri-Mix

O2 ____% N ____%

HE ____%

Rebreather Scrubber Monitor

Dive Scrubber _____ Minutes

Total Scrubber _____ Minutes

Dive partner: _____ PADI NAUI ACUC Other

Email/phone: _____ Cert. Number: _____

Sightings, Hazards, Notes, Photos, Sketches

Dive Number:	Date:
Location:	
GPS:	
Body of Water:	
Site:	

Dive Class

- Wreck
- Shore
- Reef
- River
- Ice
- Deep
- Cave
- Boat
- Certify
- Photo
- Video
- _____
- _____
- _____

Weather	☾	☁❄	☁☂	☁	☀
Air Temp C/F	-10/14	0/32	10/50	20/68	30/86	40/104
Surface Temp	-10/14	0/32	10/50	20/68	30/86	40/104
Temp @ Depth	-10/14	0/32	10/50	20/68	30/86	40/104
Surface	Calm		Choppy		Waves
Current	None				Swift
Visibility M/ft	0	7.5/25	15/50	23/75	30/100

Dive Profile

- First Dive
- Second Dive
- Third Dive

DEPTH

Surface Interval	
Starting Group	
Time In	End Group
Pressure In	Safety Stop

Plan Depth	Maximum Depth	Bottom Time	Time Out	Pressure Out

TIME

Wetsuit	**Drysuit**	**Equipment**		
Full / Shorty	Liner	Weight _____ lb kg		
_____ mm	Argon	Tank _____ cuft L		
		Pony tank _____ cuft L		

- Camera
- Lighting
- Wreck reel
- Compass
- Knife
- Flashlight
- Spear gun
- Whistle
- Sausage
- Float N Flag
- Lift bag
- Float marker

Nitrox _____ %
(for air use 21%)

MOD _____ ft

Tri-Mix

O2 _____ % N _____ %

HE _____ %

Rebreather Scrubber Monitor

Dive Scrubber _____ Minutes

Total Scrubber _____ Minutes

Dive partner: _____ PADI NAUI ACUC Other

Email/phone: _____ Cert. Number: _____

Sightings, Hazards, Notes, Photos, Sketches

DIVER'S LOG BOOK

Dive Number:	Date:
Location:	
GPS:	
Body of Water:	
Site:	

Dive Class

- ○ Wreck
- ○ Boat
- ○ Shore
- ○ Certify
- ○ Reef
- ○ Photo
- ○ River
- ○ Video
- ○ Ice
- ○ _____
- ○ Deep
- ○ _____
- ○ Cave
- ○ _____

Weather	☾	❄	☁	☀☁	☀
Air Temp C/F	-10/14	0/32	10/50	20/68	30/86	40/104
Surface Temp	-10/14	0/32	10/50	20/68	30/86	40/104
Temp @ Depth	-10/14	0/32	10/50	20/68	30/86	40/104
Surface	Calm		Choppy		Waves
Current	None				Swift
Visibility M/ft	0	7.5/25	15/50	23/75	30/100

Dive Profile

○ First Dive ○ Second Dive ○ Third Dive

DEPTH

Surface Interval	
Starting Group	
Time In	End Group
Pressure In	Safety Stop

Plan Depth	Maximum Depth	Bottom Time	Time Out	Pressure Out

TIME

Wetsuit	**Drysuit**	**Equipment**		
Full / Shorty	Liner	Weight _____ lb kg	○ Camera	○ Knife	○ Sausage
_____ mm	Argon	Tank _____ cuft L	○ Lighting	○ Flashlight	○ Float N Flag
		Pony tank ____ cuft L	○ Wreck reel	○ Spear gun	○ Lift bag
			○ Compass	○ Whistle	○ Float marker

Nitrox _____ %
(for air use 21%)

MOD _____ ft

Tri-Mix

O2 ____ % N _____ %

HE ____ %

Rebreather Scrubber Monitor

Dive Scrubber _____ Minutes

Total Scrubber _____ Minutes

Dive partner: _____ PADI NAUI ACUC Other

Email/phone: _____ Cert. Number: _____

Sightings, Hazards, Notes, Photos, Sketches

DIVER'S LOG BOOK

	Dive Number:	Date:
	Location:	
	GPS:	
	Body of Water:	
	Site:	

Dive Class

- Wreck
- Shore
- Reef
- River
- Ice
- Deep
- Cave

- Boat
- Certify
- Photo
- Video
- _____
- _____
- _____

Weather	☾	❄	☔	⛅	☀
Air Temp C/F	-10/14	0/32	10/50	20/68	30/86	40/104
Surface Temp	-10/14	0/32	10/50	20/68	30/86	40/104
Temp @ Depth	-10/14	0/32	10/50	20/68	30/86	40/104
Surface	Calm		Choppy		Waves
Current	None				Swift
Visibility M/ft	0	7.5/25	15/50	23/75	30/100

Dive Profile   ● First Dive ● Second Dive ● Third Dive

D E P T H	Surface Interval				
	Starting Group				
	Time In			End Group	
	Pressure In			Safety Stop	
	Plan Depth	Maximum Depth	Bottom Time	Time Out	Pressure Out

TIME

Wetsuit	**Drysuit**	**Equipment**		
Full / Shorty	Liner	Weight _____ lb kg	● Camera	● Knife	● Sausage
_____ mm	Argon	Tank _____ cuft L	● Lighting	● Flashlight	● Float N Flag
		Pony tank _____ cuft L	● Wreck reel	● Spear gun	● Lift bag
			● Compass	● Whistle	● Float marker

Nitrox _____% (for air use 21%) MOD_____ ft	**Tri-Mix** O2 ____% N ____% HE ____%	**Rebreather Scrubber Monitor** Dive Scrubber_____ Minutes Total Scrubber_____ Minutes

Dive partner:_____ PADI NAUI ACUC Other

Email/phone:_____ Cert. Number: _____

Sightings, Hazards, Notes, Photos, Sketches

DIVER'S LOG BOOK

Dive Number:	Date:
Location:	
GPS:	
Body of Water:	
Site:	

Dive Class

- Wreck
- Shore
- Reef
- River
- Ice
- Deep
- Cave
- Boat
- Certify
- Photo
- Video
- _____
- _____
- _____

Weather	☾	❄	🌧	⛅	☀
Air Temp C/F	-10/14	0/32	10/50	20/68	30/86	40/104
Surface Temp	-10/14	0/32	10/50	20/68	30/86	40/104
Temp @ Depth	-10/14	0/32	10/50	20/68	30/86	40/104
Surface	Calm		Choppy		Waves
Current	None				Swift
Visibility M/ft	0	7.5/25	15/50	23/75	30/100

Dive Profile

- First Dive
- Second Dive
- Third Dive

DEPTH

Surface Interval	
Starting Group	
Time In	End Group
Pressure In	Safety Stop

Plan Depth	Maximum Depth	Bottom Time	Time Out	Pressure Out

TIME

Wetsuit	**Drysuit**
Full / Shorty	Liner
_____ mm	Argon

Equipment

Weight _____ lb kg
Tank _____ cuft L
Pony tank _____ cuft L

- Camera
- Lighting
- Wreck reel
- Compass
- Knife
- Flashlight
- Spear gun
- Whistle
- Sausage
- Float N Flag
- Lift bag
- Float marker

Nitrox _____ %
(for air use 21%)

MOD_____ ft

Tri-Mix

O2 _____ % N _____ %
HE _____ %

Rebreather Scrubber Monitor

Dive Scrubber_____ Minutes
Total Scrubber _____ Minutes

Dive partner:_____ PADI NAUI ACUC Other

Email/phone: _____ Cert. Number: _____

Sightings, Hazards, Notes, Photos, Sketches

DIVER'S LOG BOOK

	Dive Number:	Date:
	Location:	
	GPS:	
	Body of Water:	
	Site:	

Dive Class

- Wreck
- Shore
- Reef
- River
- Ice
- Deep
- Cave
- Boat
- Certify
- Photo
- Video
- _____
- _____
- _____

Weather	🌙	❄️	🌧️	⛅	☀️
Air Temp C/F	-10/14	0/32	10/50	20/68	30/86	40/104
Surface Temp	-10/14	0/32	10/50	20/68	30/86	40/104
Temp @ Depth	-10/14	0/32	10/50	20/68	30/86	40/104
Surface	Calm		Choppy		Waves
Current	None				Swift
Visibility M/ft	0	7.5/25	15/50	23/75	30/100

Dive Profile   ⚪ First Dive   ⚪ Second Dive   ⚪ Third Dive

D E P T H	Surface Interval			
	Starting Group			
	Time In			End Group
	Pressure In			Safety Stop
	Plan Depth	Maximum Depth	Bottom Time	Time Out	Pressure Out

TIME

Wetsuit	**Drysuit**	**Equipment**		
Full / Shorty	Liner	Weight _____ lb kg	⚪ Camera	⚪ Knife	⚪ Sausage
_____ mm	Argon	Tank _____ cuft L	⚪ Lighting	⚪ Flashlight	⚪ Float N Flag
		Pony tank _____ cuft L	⚪ Wreck reel	⚪ Spear gun	⚪ Lift bag
			⚪ Compass	⚪ Whistle	⚪ Float marker

Nitrox _____ %	**Tri-Mix**	**Rebreather Scrubber Monitor**
(for air use 21%)	O2 ____ % N ____ %	Dive Scrubber _____ Minutes
MOD _____ ft	HE ____ %	Total Scrubber _____ Minutes

Dive partner: _____ PADI NAUI ACUC Other

Email/phone: _____ Cert. Number: _____

Sightings, Hazards, Notes, Photos, Sketches

DIVER'S LOG BOOK

	Dive Number:	Date:
	Location:	
	GPS:	
	Body of Water:	
	Site:	

Dive Class

- ○ Wreck
- ○ Boat
- ○ Shore
- ○ Certify
- ○ Reef
- ○ Photo
- ○ River
- ○ Video
- ○ Ice
- ○ _____
- ○ Deep
- ○ _____
- ○ Cave
- ○ _____

Weather	☾	❄	🌧	⛅	☀
Air Temp C/F	-10/14	0/32	10/50	20/68	30/86	40/104
Surface Temp	-10/14	0/32	10/50	20/68	30/86	40/104
Temp @ Depth	-10/14	0/32	10/50	20/68	30/86	40/104
Surface	Calm		Choppy		Waves
Current	None				Swift
Visibility M/ft	0	7.5/25	15/50	23/75	30/100

Dive Profile

○ First Dive   ○ Second Dive   ○ Third Dive

DEPTH

Surface Interval		
Starting Group		
Time In		End Group
Pressure In		Safety Stop

Plan Depth	Maximum Depth	Bottom Time	Time Out	Pressure Out

TIME

Wetsuit **Drysuit**
Full / Shorty Liner
_____ mm Argon

Equipment
Weight _____ lb kg
Tank _____ cuft L
Pony tank _____ cuft L

- ○ Camera
- ○ Knife
- ○ Sausage
- ○ Lighting
- ○ Flashlight
- ○ Float N Flag
- ○ Wreck reel
- ○ Spear gun
- ○ Lift bag
- ○ Compass
- ○ Whistle
- ○ Float marker

Nitrox _____%
(for air use 21%)

MOD _____ ft

Tri-Mix
O2 ____% N ____%
HE ____%

Rebreather Scrubber Monitor
Dive Scrubber _____ Minutes
Total Scrubber _____ Minutes

Dive partner: _____ PADI NAUI ACUC Other

Email/phone: _____ Cert. Number: _____

Sightings, Hazards, Notes, Photos, Sketches

DIVER'S LOG BOOK

	Dive Number:	Date:
	Location:	
	GPS:	
	Body of Water:	
	Site:	

Dive Class

- ○ Wreck
- ○ Boat
- ○ Shore
- ○ Certify
- ○ Reef
- ○ Photo
- ○ River
- ○ Video
- ○ Ice
- ○ _____
- ○ Deep
- ○ _____
- ○ Cave
- ○ _____

Weather	☾	❄	🌧	⛅	☀
Air Temp C/F	-10/14	0/32	10/50	20/68	30/86	40/104
Surface Temp	-10/14	0/32	10/50	20/68	30/86	40/104
Temp @ Depth	-10/14	0/32	10/50	20/68	30/86	40/104
Surface	Calm		Choppy		Waves
Current	None				Swift
Visibility M/ft	0	7.5/25	15/50	23/75	30/100

Dive Profile

○ First Dive ○ Second Dive ○ Third Dive

Surface Interval				
Starting Group				
Time In			End Group	
Pressure In			Safety Stop	
Plan Depth	Maximum Depth	Bottom Time	Time Out	Pressure Out

DEPTH

TIME

Wetsuit **Drysuit**
Full / Shorty   Liner
_____ mm   Argon

Equipment
Weight _____ lb kg
Tank _____ cuft L
Pony tank _____ cuft L

- ○ Camera
- ○ Knife
- ○ Sausage
- ○ Lighting
- ○ Flashlight
- ○ Float N Flag
- ○ Wreck reel
- ○ Spear gun
- ○ Lift bag
- ○ Compass
- ○ Whistle
- ○ Float marker

Nitrox _____ %
(for air use 21%)

MOD _____ ft

Tri-Mix
O2 _____ % N _____ %
HE _____ %

Rebreather Scrubber Monitor
Dive Scrubber _____ Minutes
Total Scrubber _____ Minutes

Dive partner: _____ PADI NAUI ACUC Other

Email/phone: _____ Cert. Number: _____

Sightings, Hazards, Notes, Photos, Sketches

DIVER'S LOG BOOK

	Dive Number:	**Date:**
	Location:	
	GPS:	
	Body of Water:	
	Site:	

Dive Class

- Wreck
- Boat
- Shore
- Certify
- Reef
- Photo
- River
- Video
- Ice
- _____
- Deep
- _____
- Cave
- _____

Weather	☾	☁❄	🌧	⛅	☀
Air Temp C/F	-10/14	0/32	10/50	20/68	30/86	40/104
Surface Temp	-10/14	0/32	10/50	20/68	30/86	40/104
Temp @ Depth	-10/14	0/32	10/50	20/68	30/86	40/104
Surface	Calm		Choppy			Waves
Current	None					Swift
Visibility M/ft	0	7.5/25	15/50	23/75	30/100

Dive Profile

- First Dive
- Second Dive
- Third Dive

D E P T H

Surface Interval	
Starting Group	
Time In	End Group
Pressure In	Safety Stop

Plan Depth	Maximum Depth	Bottom Time	Time Out	Pressure Out

TIME

Wetsuit
Full / Shorty
_____ mm

Drysuit
Liner
Argon

Equipment
Weight _____ lb kg
Tank _____ cuft L
Pony tank _____ cuft L

- Camera
- Knife
- Sausage
- Lighting
- Flashlight
- Float N Flag
- Wreck reel
- Spear gun
- Lift bag
- Compass
- Whistle
- Float marker

Nitrox _____ %
(for air use 21%)

MOD _____ ft

Tri-Mix

O2 _____ % N _____ %
HE _____ %

Rebreather Scrubber Monitor

Dive Scrubber _____ Minutes

Total Scrubber _____ Minutes

Dive partner: _____ PADI NAUI ACUC Other

Email/phone: _____ Cert. Number: _____

Sightings, Hazards, Notes, Photos, Sketches

DIVER'S LOG BOOK

Dive Number:	Date:
Location:	
GPS:	
Body of Water:	
Site:	

Dive Class

- ○ Wreck
- ○ Boat
- ○ Shore
- ○ Certify
- ○ Reef
- ○ Photo
- ○ River
- ○ Video
- ○ Ice
- ○ _____
- ○ Deep
- ○ _____
- ○ Cave
- ○ _____

Weather	☾	❄	🌧	⛅	☀
Air Temp C/F	-10/14	0/32	10/50	20/68	30/86	40/104
Surface Temp	-10/14	0/32	10/50	20/68	30/86	40/104
Temp @ Depth	-10/14	0/32	10/50	20/68	30/86	40/104
Surface	Calm		Choppy		Waves
Current	None				Swift
Visibility M/ft	0	7.5/25	15/50	23/75	30/100

Dive Profile

○ First Dive ○ Second Dive ○ Third Dive

DEPTH

Surface Interval	
Starting Group	
Time In	End Group
Pressure In	Safety Stop

Plan Depth	Maximum Depth	Bottom Time	Time Out	Pressure Out

TIME

Wetsuit **Drysuit**
Full / Shorty Liner
_____ mm Argon

Equipment
Weight _____ lb kg
Tank _____ cuft L
Pony tank _____ cuft L

- ○ Camera
- ○ Knife
- ○ Sausage
- ○ Lighting
- ○ Flashlight
- ○ Float N Flag
- ○ Wreck reel
- ○ Spear gun
- ○ Lift bag
- ○ Compass
- ○ Whistle
- ○ Float marker

Nitrox _____%
(for air use 21%)

MOD_____ft

Tri-Mix
O2 _____% N _____%
HE _____%

Rebreather Scrubber Monitor
Dive Scrubber_____ Minutes
Total Scrubber_____ Minutes

Dive partner:_____ PADI NAUI ACUC Other

Email/phone:_____ Cert. Number: _____

Sightings, Hazards, Notes, Photos, Sketches

DIVER'S LOG BOOK

Dive Number:		Date:
Location:		
GPS:		
Body of Water:		
Site:		

Dive Class

- Wreck
- Shore
- Reef
- River
- Ice
- Deep
- Cave
- Boat
- Certify
- Photo
- Video
- _____
- _____
- _____

Weather	☾	☁❄	☁☔	⛅	☀
Air Temp C/F	-10/14	0/32	10/50	20/68	30/86	40/104
Surface Temp	-10/14	0/32	10/50	20/68	30/86	40/104
Temp @ Depth	-10/14	0/32	10/50	20/68	30/86	40/104
Surface	Calm		Choppy		Waves
Current	None				Swift
Visibility M/ft	0	7.5/25	15/50	23/75	30/100

Dive Profile

- First Dive
- Second Dive
- Third Dive

DEPTH

Surface Interval		
Starting Group		
Time In		End Group
Pressure In		Safety Stop
Plan Depth	Maximum Depth	Bottom Time	Time Out	Pressure Out

TIME

Wetsuit	**Drysuit**	**Equipment**	
Full / Shorty	Liner	Weight _____ lb kg	
_____ mm	Argon	Tank _____ cuft L	
		Pony tank _____ cuft L	

- Camera
- Lighting
- Wreck reel
- Compass
- Knife
- Flashlight
- Spear gun
- Whistle
- Sausage
- Float N Flag
- Lift bag
- Float marker

Nitrox _____ %
(for air use 21%)

MOD _____ ft

Tri-Mix

O2 ____ % N ____ %

HE ____ %

Rebreather Scrubber Monitor

Dive Scrubber _____ Minutes

Total Scrubber _____ Minutes

Dive partner: _____ PADI NAUI ACUC Other

Email/phone: _____ Cert. Number: _____

Sightings, Hazards, Notes, Photos, Sketches

Dive Number:		Date:
Location:		
GPS:		
Body of Water:		
Site:		

Dive Class

- Wreck
- Shore
- Reef
- River
- Ice
- Deep
- Cave
- Boat
- Certify
- Photo
- Video
- _____
- _____
- _____

Weather	🌙	☁❄	🌧	⛅	☀
Air Temp C/F	-10/14	0/32	10/50	20/68	30/86	40/104
Surface Temp	-10/14	0/32	10/50	20/68	30/86	40/104
Temp @ Depth	-10/14	0/32	10/50	20/68	30/86	40/104
Surface	Calm		Choppy		Waves
Current	None				Swift
Visibility M/ft	0	7.5/25	15/50	23/75	30/100

Dive Profile   ● First Dive   ● Second Dive   ● Third Dive

D E P T H

Surface Interval		
Starting Group		
Time In		End Group
Pressure In		Safety Stop

Plan Depth	Maximum Depth	Bottom Time	Time Out	Pressure Out

TIME

Wetsuit **Drysuit**	**Equipment**		
Full / Shorty Liner	Weight _____ lb kg	● Camera	● Knife	● Sausage
_____ mm Argon	Tank _____ cuft L	● Lighting	● Flashlight	● Float N Flag
	Pony tank _____ cuft L	● Wreck reel	● Spear gun	● Lift bag
		● Compass	● Whistle	● Float marker

Nitrox _____% (for air use 21%) MOD_____ft	**Tri-Mix** O2 ____% N ____% HE ____%	**Rebreather Scrubber Monitor** Dive Scrubber_____ Minutes Total Scrubber_____ Minutes

Dive partner:_____ PADI NAUI ACUC Other

Email/phone:_____ Cert. Number: _____

Sightings, Hazards, Notes, Photos, Sketches

DIVER'S LOG BOOK

Dive Number:	Date:

Location:

GPS:

Body of Water:

Site:

Dive Class

- Wreck
- Shore
- Reef
- River
- Ice
- Deep
- Cave
- Boat
- Certify
- Photo
- Video
- _____
- _____
- _____

Weather	☾	❄	☔	⛅	☀
Air Temp C/F	-10/14	0/32	10/50	20/68	30/86	40/104
Surface Temp	-10/14	0/32	10/50	20/68	30/86	40/104
Temp @ Depth	-10/14	0/32	10/50	20/68	30/86	40/104
Surface	Calm		Choppy		Waves
Current	None				Swift
Visibility M/ft	0	7.5/25	15/50	23/75	30/100

Dive Profile

- First Dive
- Second Dive
- Third Dive

DEPTH

Surface Interval	
Starting Group	
Time In	End Group
Pressure In	Safety Stop
Plan Depth	Maximum Depth	Bottom Time	Time Out	Pressure Out

TIME

Wetsuit	**Drysuit**	**Equipment**
Full / Shorty	Liner	Weight _____ lb kg
_____ mm	Argon	Tank _____ cuft L
		Pony tank _____ cuft L

- Camera
- Lighting
- Wreck reel
- Compass
- Knife
- Flashlight
- Spear gun
- Whistle
- Sausage
- Float N Flag
- Lift bag
- Float marker

Nitrox _____ %
(for air use 21%)

MOD _____ ft

Tri-Mix

O2 _____ % N _____ %

HE _____ %

Rebreather Scrubber Monitor

Dive Scrubber _____ Minutes

Total Scrubber _____ Minutes

Dive partner: _____ PADI NAUI ACUC Other

Email/phone: _____ Cert. Number: _____

Sightings, Hazards, Notes, Photos, Sketches

DIVER'S LOG BOOK

Dive Number:	Date:
Location:	
GPS:	
Body of Water:	
Site:	

Dive Class

- Wreck
- Boat
- Shore
- Certify
- Reef
- Photo
- River
- Video
- Ice
- _____
- Deep
- _____
- Cave
- _____

Weather	🌙	☁❄	🌧	⛅	☀
Air Temp C/F	-10/14	0/32	10/50	20/68	30/86	40/104
Surface Temp	-10/14	0/32	10/50	20/68	30/86	40/104
Temp @ Depth	-10/14	0/32	10/50	20/68	30/86	40/104
Surface	Calm		Choppy		Waves
Current	None				Swift
Visibility M/ft	0	7.5/25	15/50	23/75	30/100

Dive Profile

- First Dive
- Second Dive
- Third Dive

DEPTH

Surface Interval				
Starting Group				
Time In				End Group
Pressure In				Safety Stop
Plan Depth	Maximum Depth	Bottom Time	Time Out	Pressure Out

TIME

Wetsuit	**Drysuit**	**Equipment**
Full / Shorty	Liner	Weight _____ lb kg
_____ mm	Argon	Tank _____ cuft L
		Pony tank _____ cuft L

- Camera
- Knife
- Sausage
- Lighting
- Flashlight
- Float N Flag
- Wreck reel
- Spear gun
- Lift bag
- Compass
- Whistle
- Float marker

Nitrox _____ % (for air use 21%) MOD _____ ft	**Tri-Mix** O2 _____% N _____% HE _____%	**Rebreather Scrubber Monitor** Dive Scrubber _____ Minutes Total Scrubber _____ Minutes

Dive partner: _____ PADI NAUI ACUC Other

Email/phone: _____ Cert. Number: _____

Sightings, Hazards, Notes, Photos, Sketches

DIVER'S LOG BOOK

Dive Number:		Date:
Location:		
GPS:		
Body of Water:		
Site:		

Dive Class

- Wreck
- Boat
- Shore
- Certify
- Reef
- Photo
- River
- Video
- Ice
- _____
- Deep
- _____
- Cave
- _____

Weather	☾	☁❄	☁🌧	⛅	☀
Air Temp C/F	-10/14	0/32	10/50	20/68	30/86	40/104
Surface Temp	-10/14	0/32	10/50	20/68	30/86	40/104
Temp @ Depth	-10/14	0/32	10/50	20/68	30/86	40/104
Surface	Calm		Choppy		Waves
Current	None				Swift
Visibility M/ft	0	7.5/25	15/50	23/75	30/100

Dive Profile

- First Dive
- Second Dive
- Third Dive

DEPTH

Surface Interval			
Starting Group			
Time In			End Group
Pressure In			Safety Stop
Plan Depth	Maximum Depth	Bottom Time	Time Out	Pressure Out

TIME

Wetsuit	**Drysuit**	**Equipment**		
Full / Shorty	Liner	Weight _____ lb kg	● Camera	● Knife	● Sausage
_____ mm	Argon	Tank _____ cuft L	● Lighting	● Flashlight	● Float N Flag
		Pony tank _____ cuft L	● Wreck reel	● Spear gun	● Lift bag
			● Compass	● Whistle	● Float marker

Nitrox _____ % (for air use 21%)	**Tri-Mix**	**Rebreather Scrubber Monitor**
	O2 ____ % N ____ %	Dive Scrubber _____ Minutes
MOD _____ ft	HE ____ %	Total Scrubber _____ Minutes

Dive partner: _____ PADI NAUI ACUC Other

Email/phone: _____ Cert. Number: _____

Sightings, Hazards, Notes, Photos, Sketches

DIVER'S LOG BOOK

Dive Number:		Date:
Location:		
GPS:		
Body of Water:		
Site:		

Dive Class

- Wreck
- Boat
- Shore
- Certify
- Reef
- Photo
- River
- Video
- Ice
- _____
- Deep
- _____
- Cave
- _____

Weather	☾	❄	🌧	⛅	☀
Air Temp C/F	-10/14	0/32	10/50	20/68	30/86	40/104
Surface Temp	-10/14	0/32	10/50	20/68	30/86	40/104
Temp @ Depth	-10/14	0/32	10/50	20/68	30/86	40/104
Surface	Calm		Choppy		Waves
Current	None				Swift
Visibility M/ft	0	7.5/25	15/50	23/75	30/100

Dive Profile

- First Dive
- Second Dive
- Third Dive

D E P T H	Surface Interval		
	Starting Group		
	Time In		End Group
	Pressure In		Safety Stop
	Plan Depth	Maximum Depth	Bottom Time	Time Out	Pressure Out

TIME

Wetsuit	**Drysuit**	**Equipment**		Camera	Knife	Sausage
Full / Shorty	Liner	Weight _____ lb kg		Lighting	Flashlight	Float N Flag
_____ mm	Argon	Tank _____ cuft L		Wreck reel	Spear gun	Lift bag
		Pony tank _____ cuft L		Compass	Whistle	Float marker

Nitrox _____%
(for air use 21%)

MOD_____ft

Tri-Mix

O2 _____% N _____%

HE _____%

Rebreather Scrubber Monitor

Dive Scrubber_____ Minutes

Total Scrubber _____ Minutes

Dive partner:_____ PADI NAUI ACUC Other

Email/phone: _____ Cert. Number: _____

Sightings, Hazards, Notes, Photos, Sketches

Dive Number:		Date:
Location:		
GPS:		
Body of Water:		
Site:		

Dive Class

- Wreck
- Shore
- Reef
- River
- Ice
- Deep
- Cave
- Boat
- Certify
- Photo
- Video
- _____
- _____
- _____

Weather	☾	❄	⛈	⛅	☀	
Air Temp C/F	-10/14	0/32	10/50	20/68	30/86	40/104
Surface Temp	-10/14	0/32	10/50	20/68	30/86	40/104
Temp @ Depth	-10/14	0/32	10/50	20/68	30/86	40/104
Surface	Calm		Choppy			Waves
Current	None					Swift
Visibility M/ft	0	7.5/25	15/50		23/75	30/100

Dive Profile

- First Dive
- Second Dive
- Third Dive

DEPTH

Surface Interval	
Starting Group	
Time In	End Group
Pressure In	Safety Stop

Plan Depth	Maximum Depth	Bottom Time	Time Out	Pressure Out

TIME

Wetsuit	**Drysuit**	**Equipment**		
Full / Shorty	Liner	Weight _____ lb kg		
_____ mm	Argon	Tank _____ cuft L		
		Pony tank _____ cuft L		

- Camera
- Lighting
- Wreck reel
- Compass
- Knife
- Flashlight
- Spear gun
- Whistle
- Sausage
- Float N Flag
- Lift bag
- Float marker

Nitrox _____ %
(for air use 21%)

MOD _____ ft

Tri-Mix

O2 _____ %   N _____ %

HE _____ %

Rebreather Scrubber Monitor

Dive Scrubber _____ Minutes

Total Scrubber _____ Minutes

Dive partner: _____ PADI NAUI ACUC Other

Email/phone: _____ Cert. Number: _____

Sightings, Hazards, Notes, Photos, Sketches

Dive Number:		Date:	
Location:			
GPS:			
Body of Water:			
Site:			

Dive Class

- Wreck
- Shore
- Reef
- River
- Ice
- Deep
- Cave
- Boat
- Certify
- Photo
- Video
- _____
- _____
- _____

Weather	☾	❄	🌧	⛅	☀
Air Temp C/F	-10/14	0/32	10/50	20/68	30/86	40/104
Surface Temp	-10/14	0/32	10/50	20/68	30/86	40/104
Temp @ Depth	-10/14	0/32	10/50	20/68	30/86	40/104
Surface	Calm		Choppy		Waves
Current	None				Swift
Visibility M/ft	0	7.5/25	15/50	23/75	30/100

Dive Profile

○ First Dive ○ Second Dive ○ Third Dive

DEPTH

Surface Interval	
Starting Group	
Time In	
Pressure In	

| | | End Group |
| | | Safety Stop |

| Plan Depth | Maximum Depth | Bottom Time | Time Out | Pressure Out |

TIME

Wetsuit	**Drysuit**	**Equipment**
Full / Shorty	Liner	Weight _____ lb kg
_____ mm	Argon	Tank _____ cuft L
		Pony tank _____ cuft L

- Camera
- Lighting
- Wreck reel
- Compass
- Knife
- Flashlight
- Spear gun
- Whistle
- Sausage
- Float N Flag
- Lift bag
- Float marker

Nitrox _____ %
(for air use 21%)

MOD _____ ft

Tri-Mix

O2 ____ % N ____ %

HE ____ %

Rebreather Scrubber Monitor

Dive Scrubber _____ Minutes

Total Scrubber _____ Minutes

Dive partner: _____ PADI NAUI ACUC Other

Email/phone: _____ Cert. Number: _____

Sightings, Hazards, Notes, Photos, Sketches

DIVER'S LOG BOOK

	Dive Number:	Date:
	Location:	
	GPS:	
	Body of Water:	
	Site:	

Dive Class

● Wreck	● Boat
● Shore	● Certify
● Reef	● Photo
● River	● Video
● Ice	● _____
● Deep	● _____
● Cave	● _____

Weather	☾	☁❄	☁🌧	⛅	☀
Air Temp C/F	-10/14	0/32	10/50	20/68	30/86	40/104
Surface Temp	-10/14	0/32	10/50	20/68	30/86	40/104
Temp @ Depth	-10/14	0/32	10/50	20/68	30/86	40/104
Surface	Calm		Choppy		Waves
Current	None				Swift
Visibility M/ft	0	7.5/25	15/50	23/75	30/100

Dive Profile   ● First Dive   ● Second Dive   ● Third Dive

DEPTH

Surface Interval	
Starting Group	
Time In	End Group
Pressure In	Safety Stop

Plan Depth	Maximum Depth	Bottom Time	Time Out	Pressure Out

TIME

Wetsuit	**Drysuit**	**Equipment**		
Full / Shorty	Liner	Weight _____ lb kg	● Camera	● Knife	● Sausage
_____ mm	Argon	Tank _____ cuft L	● Lighting	● Flashlight	● Float N Flag
		Pony tank _____ cuft L	● Wreck reel	● Spear gun	● Lift bag
			● Compass	● Whistle	● Float marker

Nitrox _____%	**Tri-Mix**	**Rebreather Scrubber Monitor**
(for air use 21%)	O2 _____% N _____%	Dive Scrubber_____ Minutes
MOD_____ft	HE _____%	Total Scrubber _____ Minutes

Dive partner:_____ PADI NAUI ACUC Other

Email/phone:_____ Cert. Number: _____

Sightings, Hazards, Notes, Photos, Sketches

DIVER'S LOG BOOK

	Dive Number:		Date:
	Location:		
	GPS:		
	Body of Water:		
	Site:		

Dive Class

- Wreck
- Shore
- Reef
- River
- Ice
- Deep
- Cave
- Boat
- Certify
- Photo
- Video
- _____
- _____
- _____

Weather	(	☁❄❄	🌧	☁	☀
Air Temp C/F	-10/14	0/32	10/50	20/68	30/86	40/104
Surface Temp	-10/14	0/32	10/50	20/68	30/86	40/104
Temp @ Depth	-10/14	0/32	10/50	20/68	30/86	40/104
Surface	Calm		Choppy		Waves
Current	None				Swift
Visibility M/ft	0	7.5/25	15/50	23/75	30/100

Dive Profile

- First Dive
- Second Dive
- Third Dive

DEPTH

Surface Interval	
Starting Group	
Time In		End Group
Pressure In		Safety Stop

Plan Depth	Maximum Depth	Bottom Time	Time Out	Pressure Out

TIME

Wetsuit	**Drysuit**	**Equipment**		
Full / Shorty	Liner	Weight _____ lb kg	○ Camera	○ Knife	○ Sausage
_____ mm	Argon	Tank _____ cuft L	○ Lighting	○ Flashlight	○ Float N Flag
		Pony tank _____ cuft L	○ Wreck reel	○ Spear gun	○ Lift bag
			○ Compass	○ Whistle	○ Float marker

Nitrox _____ % (for air use 21%)	**Tri-Mix**	**Rebreather Scrubber Monitor**
MOD _____ ft	O2 ____% N ____% HE ____%	Dive Scrubber _____ Minutes Total Scrubber _____ Minutes

Dive partner: _____ PADI NAUI ACUC Other

Email/phone: _____ Cert. Number: _____

Sightings, Hazards, Notes, Photos, Sketches

	Dive Number:	Date:
	Location:	
	GPS:	
	Body of Water:	
	Site:	

Dive Class

- Wreck
- Shore
- Reef
- River
- Ice
- Deep
- Cave
- Boat
- Certify
- Photo
- Video
- _____
- _____
- _____

Weather	☾	❄	🌧	☁	☀
Air Temp C/F	-10/14	0/32	10/50	20/68	30/86	40/104
Surface Temp	-10/14	0/32	10/50	20/68	30/86	40/104
Temp @ Depth	-10/14	0/32	10/50	20/68	30/86	40/104
Surface	Calm	Choppy		Waves
Current	None			Swift
Visibility M/ft	0	7.5/25	15/50	23/75	30/100

Dive Profile

- First Dive
- Second Dive
- Third Dive

D E P T H

Surface Interval		
Starting Group		
Time In		End Group
Pressure In		Safety Stop
Plan Depth	Maximum Depth	Bottom Time	Time Out	Pressure Out

TIME

Wetsuit	**Drysuit**
Full / Shorty	Liner
_____ mm	Argon

Equipment

Weight _____ lb kg
Tank _____ cuft L
Pony tank _____ cuft L

- Camera
- Lighting
- Wreck reel
- Compass
- Knife
- Flashlight
- Spear gun
- Whistle
- Sausage
- Float N Flag
- Lift bag
- Float marker

Nitrox _____%
(for air use 21%)

MOD _____ ft

Tri-Mix

O2 _____% N _____%
HE _____%

Rebreather Scrubber Monitor

Dive Scrubber _____ Minutes
Total Scrubber _____ Minutes

Dive partner: _____ PADI NAUI ACUC Other

Email/phone: _____ Cert. Number: _____

Sightings, Hazards, Notes, Photos, Sketches

DIVER'S LOG BOOK

	Dive Number:	Date:
	Location:	
	GPS:	
	Body of Water:	
	Site:	

Dive Class		Weather	🌙	☁❄	🌧	⛅	☀
○ Wreck	○ Boat	Air Temp C/F	-10/14	0/32	10/50	20/68	30/86	40/104
○ Shore	○ Certify	Surface Temp	-10/14	0/32	10/50	20/68	30/86	40/104
○ Reef	○ Photo	Temp @ Depth	-10/14	0/32	10/50	20/68	30/86	40/104
○ River	○ Video	Surface	Calm		Choppy		Waves
○ Ice	○ _____	Current	None				Swift
○ Deep	○ _____	Visibility M/ft	0	7.5/25	15/50	23/75	30/100
○ Cave	○ _____						

Dive Profile   ○ First Dive   ○ Second Dive   ○ Third Dive

D E P T H	Surface Interval			
	Starting Group			
	Time In			End Group
	Pressure In			Safety Stop
	Plan Depth	Maximum Depth	Bottom Time	Time Out	Pressure Out

TIME

Wetsuit	**Drysuit**	**Equipment**			
Full / Shorty	Liner	Weight _____ lb kg	○ Camera	○ Knife	○ Sausage
_____ mm	Argon	Tank _____ cuft L	○ Lighting	○ Flashlight	○ Float N Flag
		Pony tank _____ cuft L	○ Wreck reel	○ Spear gun	○ Lift bag
			○ Compass	○ Whistle	○ Float marker

Nitrox _____% (for air use 21%)	**Tri-Mix**	**Rebreather Scrubber Monitor**
MOD _____ ft	O2 ___% N ___%	Dive Scrubber _____ Minutes
	HE ___%	Total Scrubber _____ Minutes

Dive partner: _____ PADI NAUI ACUC Other

Email/phone: _____ Cert. Number: _____

Sightings, Hazards, Notes, Photos, Sketches

DIVER'S LOG BOOK

Dive Number:		Date:
Location:		
GPS:		
Body of Water:		
Site:		

Dive Class

○ Wreck	○ Boat
○ Shore	○ Certify
○ Reef	○ Photo
○ River	○ Video
○ Ice	○ _____
○ Deep	○ _____
○ Cave	○ _____

Weather	☾	❄	☔	☁	☀
Air Temp C/F	-10/14	0/32	10/50	20/68	30/86	40/104
Surface Temp	-10/14	0/32	10/50	20/68	30/86	40/104
Temp @ Depth	-10/14	0/32	10/50	20/68	30/86	40/104
Surface	Calm		Choppy			Waves
Current	None					Swift
Visibility M/ft	0	7.5/25	15/50	23/75	30/100

Dive Profile   ○ First Dive   ○ Second Dive   ○ Third Dive

D E P T H

Surface Interval	
Starting Group	
Time In	End Group
Pressure In	Safety Stop

Plan Depth	Maximum Depth	Bottom Time	Time Out	Pressure Out

TIME

Wetsuit	**Drysuit**	**Equipment**		
Full / Shorty	Liner	Weight _____ lb kg	○ Camera	○ Knife	○ Sausage
_____ mm	Argon	Tank _____ cuft L	○ Lighting	○ Flashlight	○ Float N Flag
		Pony tank _____ cuft L	○ Wreck reel	○ Spear gun	○ Lift bag
			○ Compass	○ Whistle	○ Float marker

Nitrox _____ %	**Tri-Mix**	**Rebreather Scrubber Monitor**
(for air use 21%)	O2 ____ % N ____ %	Dive Scrubber_____ Minutes
MOD_____ ft	HE ____ %	Total Scrubber_____ Minutes

Dive partner:_____ PADI NAUI ACUC Other

Email/phone:_____ Cert. Number: _____

Sightings, Hazards, Notes, Photos, Sketches

DIVER'S LOG BOOK

Dive Number:	Date:
Location:	
GPS:	
Body of Water:	
Site:	

Dive Class

- ○ Wreck
- ○ Shore
- ○ Reef
- ○ River
- ○ Ice
- ○ Deep
- ○ Cave
- ○ Boat
- ○ Certify
- ○ Photo
- ○ Video
- ○ _____
- ○ _____
- ○ _____

Weather	☾	❅	🌧	⛅	☀
Air Temp C/F	-10/14	0/32	10/50	20/68	30/86	40/104
Surface Temp	-10/14	0/32	10/50	20/68	30/86	40/104
Temp @ Depth	-10/14	0/32	10/50	20/68	30/86	40/104
Surface	Calm		Choppy		Waves
Current	None				Swift
Visibility M/ft	0	7.5/25	15/50	23/75	30/100

Dive Profile

○ First Dive   ○ Second Dive   ○ Third Dive

D E P T H	Surface Interval			
	Starting Group			
	Time In			End Group
	Pressure In			Safety Stop
	Plan Depth	Maximum Depth	Bottom Time	Time Out	Pressure Out

TIME

Wetsuit	**Drysuit**
Full / Shorty	Liner
____ mm	Argon

Equipment

Weight _____ lb kg
Tank _____ cuft L
Pony tank _____ cuft L

- ○ Camera
- ○ Lighting
- ○ Wreck reel
- ○ Compass
- ○ Knife
- ○ Flashlight
- ○ Spear gun
- ○ Whistle
- ○ Sausage
- ○ Float N Flag
- ○ Lift bag
- ○ Float marker

Nitrox _____%
(for air use 21%)

MOD_____ft

Tri-Mix

O2 ____% N ____%
HE ____%

Rebreather Scrubber Monitor

Dive Scrubber_____ Minutes
Total Scrubber _____ Minutes

Dive partner:_____ PADI NAUI ACUC Other

Email/phone: _____ Cert. Number: _____

Sightings, Hazards, Notes, Photos, Sketches

DIVER'S LOG BOOK

Dive Number:		Date:
Location:		
GPS:		
Body of Water:		
Site:		

Dive Class

- ⦿ Wreck
- ⦿ Shore
- ⦿ Reef
- ⦿ River
- ⦿ Ice
- ⦿ Deep
- ⦿ Cave
- ⦿ Boat
- ⦿ Certify
- ⦿ Photo
- ⦿ Video
- ⦿ _____
- ⦿ _____
- ⦿ _____

Weather	☾	❄	🌧	☁	☀
Air Temp C/F	-10/14	0/32	10/50	20/68	30/86	40/104
Surface Temp	-10/14	0/32	10/50	20/68	30/86	40/104
Temp @ Depth	-10/14	0/32	10/50	20/68	30/86	40/104
Surface	Calm		Choppy		Waves
Current	None				Swift
Visibility M/ft	0	7.5/25	15/50	23/75	30/100

Dive Profile

⦿ First Dive ⦿ Second Dive ⦿ Third Dive

DEPTH

Surface Interval	
Starting Group	
Time In	End Group
Pressure In	Safety Stop

Plan Depth	Maximum Depth	Bottom Time	Time Out	Pressure Out

TIME

Wetsuit **Drysuit**
Full / Shorty   Liner
_____ mm   Argon

Equipment
Weight _____ lb kg
Tank _____ cuft L
Pony tank _____ cuft L

- ⦿ Camera
- ⦿ Lighting
- ⦿ Wreck reel
- ⦿ Compass
- ⦿ Knife
- ⦿ Flashlight
- ⦿ Spear gun
- ⦿ Whistle
- ⦿ Sausage
- ⦿ Float N Flag
- ⦿ Lift bag
- ⦿ Float marker

Nitrox _____ %
(for air use 21%)

MOD _____ ft

Tri-Mix
O2 _____ % N _____ %
HE _____ %

Rebreather Scrubber Monitor
Dive Scrubber _____ Minutes
Total Scrubber _____ Minutes

Dive partner: _____ PADI NAUI ACUC Other

Email/phone: _____ Cert. Number: _____

Sightings, Hazards, Notes, Photos, Sketches

DIVER'S LOG BOOK

Dive Number:		Date:
Location:		
GPS:		
Body of Water:		
Site:		

Dive Class

- Wreck
- Shore
- Reef
- River
- Ice
- Deep
- Cave

- Boat
- Certify
- Photo
- Video
- _____
- _____
- _____

Weather	☾	☁❄	☁🌧	☀☁	☀
Air Temp C/F	-10/14	0/32	10/50	20/68	30/86	40/104
Surface Temp	-10/14	0/32	10/50	20/68	30/86	40/104
Temp @ Depth	-10/14	0/32	10/50	20/68	30/86	40/104
Surface	Calm		Choppy		Waves
Current	None				Swift
Visibility M/ft	0	7.5/25	15/50	23/75	30/100

Dive Profile   ● First Dive   ● Second Dive   ● Third Dive

DEPTH

Surface Interval	
Starting Group	
Time In		End Group
Pressure In		Safety Stop

Plan Depth	Maximum Depth	Bottom Time	Time Out	Pressure Out

TIME

Wetsuit	**Drysuit**	**Equipment**
Full / Shorty	Liner	Weight _____ lb kg
_____ mm	Argon	Tank _____ cuft L
		Pony tank _____ cuft L

- Camera
- Lighting
- Wreck reel
- Compass

- Knife
- Flashlight
- Spear gun
- Whistle

- Sausage
- Float N Flag
- Lift bag
- Float marker

Nitrox _____ %
(for air use 21%)

MOD_____ ft

Tri-Mix

O2 ____ %   N ____ %

HE ____ %

Rebreather Scrubber Monitor

Dive Scrubber_____ Minutes

Total Scrubber_____ Minutes

Dive partner:_____ PADI NAUI ACUC Other

Email/phone:_____ Cert. Number: _____

Sightings, Hazards, Notes, Photos, Sketches

	Dive Number:	Date:
	Location:	
	GPS:	
	Body of Water:	
	Site:	

Dive Class

Wreck	Boat
Shore	Certify
Reef	Photo
River	Video
Ice	_____
Deep	_____
Cave	_____

Weather	☽	❄	☔	⛅	☀
Air Temp C/F	-10/14	0/32	10/50	20/68	30/86	40/104
Surface Temp	-10/14	0/32	10/50	20/68	30/86	40/104
Temp @ Depth	-10/14	0/32	10/50	20/68	30/86	40/104
Surface	Calm		Choppy		Waves
Current	None				Swift
Visibility M/ft	0	7.5/25	15/50	23/75	30/100

Dive Profile   First Dive   Second Dive   Third Dive

DEPTH

Surface Interval	
Starting Group	
Time In	End Group
Pressure In	Safety Stop

Plan Depth	Maximum Depth	Bottom Time	Time Out	Pressure Out

TIME

Wetsuit **Drysuit**

Full / Shorty   Liner

_____ mm   Argon

Equipment

Weight _____ lb kg

Tank _____ cuft L

Pony tank _____ cuft L

Camera	Knife	Sausage
Lighting	Flashlight	Float N Flag
Wreck reel	Spear gun	Lift bag
Compass	Whistle	Float marker

Nitrox _____%
(for air use 21%)

MOD_____ft

Tri-Mix

O2 _____% N _____%

HE _____%

Rebreather Scrubber Monitor

Dive Scrubber_____ Minutes

Total Scrubber_____ Minutes

Dive partner:_____ PADI NAUI ACUC Other

Email/phone:_____ Cert. Number: _____

Sightings, Hazards, Notes, Photos, Sketches

DIVER'S LOG BOOK

Dive Number:		Date:
Location:		
GPS:		
Body of Water:		
Site:		

Dive Class

- Wreck
- Shore
- Reef
- River
- Ice
- Deep
- Cave
- Boat
- Certify
- Photo
- Video
- _____
- _____
- _____

Weather	☾	☁❄	☁🌧	⛅	☀
Air Temp C/F	-10/14	0/32	10/50	20/68	30/86	40/104
Surface Temp	-10/14	0/32	10/50	20/68	30/86	40/104
Temp @ Depth	-10/14	0/32	10/50	20/68	30/86	40/104
Surface	Calm		Choppy		Waves
Current	None				Swift
Visibility M/ft	0	7.5/25	15/50	23/75	30/100

Dive Profile   ● First Dive   ● Second Dive   ● Third Dive

D E P T H	Surface Interval				
	Starting Group				
	Time In				End Group
	Pressure In				Safety Stop
	Plan Depth	Maximum Depth	Bottom Time	Time Out	Pressure Out

TIME

Wetsuit	**Drysuit**	**Equipment**		
Full / Shorty	Liner	Weight _____ lb kg	● Camera	● Knife	● Sausage
____ mm	Argon	Tank _____ cuft L	● Lighting	● Flashlight	● Float N Flag
		Pony tank _____ cuft L	● Wreck reel	● Spear gun	● Lift bag
			● Compass	● Whistle	● Float marker

Nitrox _____%
(for air use 21%)

MOD_____ft

Tri-Mix

O2 ____% N ____%

HE ____%

Rebreather Scrubber Monitor

Dive Scrubber_____ Minutes

Total Scrubber_____ Minutes

Dive partner:_____ PADI   NAUI   ACUC   Other

Email/phone:_____ Cert. Number: _____

Sightings, Hazards, Notes, Photos, Sketches

Dive Number:		Date:
Location:		
GPS:		
Body of Water:		
Site:		

Dive Class

- Wreck
- Shore
- Reef
- River
- Ice
- Deep
- Cave

- Boat
- Certify
- Photo
- Video
- _____
- _____
- _____

Weather	☾	❄	🌧	⛅	☀
Air Temp C/F	-10/14	0/32	10/50	20/68	30/86	40/104
Surface Temp	-10/14	0/32	10/50	20/68	30/86	40/104
Temp @ Depth	-10/14	0/32	10/50	20/68	30/86	40/104
Surface	Calm	-	Choppy		Waves
Current	None				Swift
Visibility M/ft	0	7.5/25	15/50	23/75	30/100

Dive Profile

First Dive Second Dive Third Dive

DEPTH

Surface Interval				
Starting Group				
Time In			End Group	
Pressure In			Safety Stop	
Plan Depth	Maximum Depth	Bottom Time	Time Out	Pressure Out

TIME

Wetsuit
Full / Shorty
_____ mm

Drysuit
Liner
Argon

Equipment
Weight _____ lb kg
Tank _____ cuft L
Pony tank _____ cuft L

- Camera
- Lighting
- Wreck reel
- Compass

- Knife
- Flashlight
- Spear gun
- Whistle

- Sausage
- Float N Flag
- Lift bag
- Float marker

Nitrox _____ %
(for air use 21%)

MOD _____ ft

Tri-Mix
O2 _____ % N _____ %
HE _____ %

Rebreather Scrubber Monitor
Dive Scrubber _____ Minutes
Total Scrubber _____ Minutes

Dive partner: _____ PADI NAUI ACUC Other

Email/phone: _____ Cert. Number: _____

Sightings, Hazards, Notes, Photos, Sketches

DIVER'S LOG BOOK

	Dive Number:	Date:
	Location:	
	GPS:	
	Body of Water:	
	Site:	

Dive Class

- ○ Wreck
- ○ Shore
- ○ Reef
- ○ River
- ○ Ice
- ○ Deep
- ○ Cave
- ○ Boat
- ○ Certify
- ○ Photo
- ○ Video
- ○ _____
- ○ _____
- ○ _____

Weather	☾	❄	☔	⛅	☀
Air Temp C/F	-10/14	0/32	10/50	20/68	30/86	40/104
Surface Temp	-10/14	0/32	10/50	20/68	30/86	40/104
Temp @ Depth	-10/14	0/32	10/50	20/68	30/86	40/104
Surface	Calm		Choppy		Waves
Current	None				Swift
Visibility M/ft	0	7.5/25	15/50	23/75	30/100

Dive Profile   ○ First Dive   ○ Second Dive   ○ Third Dive

D E P T H

Surface Interval		
Starting Group		
Time In		End Group
Pressure In		Safety Stop

Plan Depth	Maximum Depth	Bottom Time	Time Out	Pressure Out

TIME

Wetsuit	**Drysuit**	**Equipment**	
Full / Shorty	Liner	Weight _____ lb kg	○ Camera ○ Knife ○ Sausage
_____ mm	Argon	Tank _____ cuft L	○ Lighting ○ Flashlight ○ Float N Flag
		Pony tank _____ cuft L	○ Wreck reel ○ Spear gun ○ Lift bag
			○ Compass ○ Whistle ○ Float marker

Nitrox _____ % (for air use 21%)	**Tri-Mix**	**Rebreather Scrubber Monitor**
	O2 _____ % N _____ %	Dive Scrubber _____ Minutes
MOD _____ ft	HE _____ %	Total Scrubber _____ Minutes

Dive partner: _____   PADI   NAUI   ACUC   Other

Email/phone: _____   Cert. Number: _____

Sightings, Hazards, Notes, Photos, Sketches

DIVER'S LOG BOOK

	Dive Number:	Date:
	Location:	
	GPS:	
	Body of Water:	
	Site:	

Dive Class		Weather	🌙	❄️	🌧️	⛅	☀️
⚪ Wreck	⚪ Boat	Air Temp C/F	-10/14	0/32	10/50	20/68	30/86	40/104
⚪ Shore	⚪ Certify	Surface Temp	-10/14	0/32	10/50	20/68	30/86	40/104
⚪ Reef	⚪ Photo	Temp @ Depth	-10/14	0/32	10/50	20/68	30/86	40/104
⚪ River	⚪ Video	Surface	Calm		Choppy		Waves
⚪ Ice	⚪ _____	Current	None				Swift
⚪ Deep	⚪ _____	Visibility M/ft	0	7.5/25	15/50	23/75	30/100
⚪ Cave	⚪ _____						

Dive Profile ⚪ First Dive ⚪ Second Dive ⚪ Third Dive

D E P T H	Surface Interval				
	Starting Group				
	Time In			End Group	
	Pressure In			Safety Stop	
	Plan Depth	Maximum Depth	Bottom Time	Time Out	Pressure Out

TIME

Wetsuit	**Drysuit**	**Equipment**		
Full / Shorty	Liner	Weight _____ lb kg	⚪ Camera	⚪ Knife	⚪ Sausage
_____ mm	Argon	Tank _____ cuft L	⚪ Lighting	⚪ Flashlight	⚪ Float N Flag
		Pony tank _____ cuft L	⚪ Wreck reel	⚪ Spear gun	⚪ Lift bag
			⚪ Compass	⚪ Whistle	⚪ Float marker

Nitrox _____ %	**Tri-Mix**	**Rebreather Scrubber Monitor**
(for air use 21%)	O2 ____ % N ____ %	Dive Scrubber _____ Minutes
MOD _____ ft	HE ____ %	Total Scrubber _____ Minutes

Dive partner: _____ PADI   NAUI   ACUC   Other

Email/phone: _____ Cert. Number: _____

Sightings, Hazards, Notes, Photos, Sketches

DIVER'S LOG BOOK

Dive Number:	Date:

Location:
GPS:
Body of Water:
Site:

Dive Class

- Wreck
- Shore
- Reef
- River
- Ice
- Deep
- Cave
- Boat
- Certify
- Photo
- Video
- _____
- _____
- _____

Weather	☾	❄	☔	⛅	☀
Air Temp C/F	-10/14	0/32	10/50	20/68	30/86	40/104
Surface Temp	-10/14	0/32	10/50	20/68	30/86	40/104
Temp @ Depth	-10/14	0/32	10/50	20/68	30/86	40/104
Surface	Calm		Choppy			Waves
Current	None					Swift
Visibility M/ft	0	7.5/25		15/50	23/75	30/100

Dive Profile

- First Dive
- Second Dive
- Third Dive

DEPTH

Surface Interval		
Starting Group		
Time In		End Group
Pressure In		Safety Stop
Plan Depth	Maximum Depth	Bottom Time	Time Out	Pressure Out

TIME

Wetsuit	**Drysuit**	**Equipment**
Full / Shorty	Liner	Weight _____ lb kg
_____ mm	Argon	Tank _____ cuft L
		Pony tank _____ cuft L

- Camera
- Lighting
- Wreck reel
- Compass
- Knife
- Flashlight
- Spear gun
- Whistle
- Sausage
- Float N Flag
- Lift bag
- Float marker

Nitrox _____ %
(for air use 21%)

MOD _____ ft

Tri-Mix

O2 _____ % N _____ %

HE _____ %

Rebreather Scrubber Monitor

Dive Scrubber _____ Minutes

Total Scrubber _____ Minutes

Dive partner: _____ PADI NAUI ACUC Other

Email/phone: _____ Cert. Number: _____

Sightings, Hazards, Notes, Photos, Sketches

Dive Number:	Date:
Location:	
GPS:	
Body of Water:	
Site:	

Dive Class

- Wreck
- Shore
- Reef
- River
- Ice
- Deep
- Cave
- Boat
- Certify
- Photo
- Video
- _____
- _____
- _____

Weather	☾	☁❄	🌧	⛅	☀
Air Temp C/F	-10/14	0/32	10/50	20/68	30/86	40/104
Surface Temp	-10/14	0/32	10/50	20/68	30/86	40/104
Temp @ Depth	-10/14	0/32	10/50	20/68	30/86	40/104
Surface	Calm		Choppy		Waves
Current	None				Swift
Visibility M/ft	0	7.5/25	15/50	23/75	30/100

Dive Profile

- First Dive
- Second Dive
- Third Dive

DEPTH

Surface Interval	
Starting Group	
Time In	End Group
Pressure In	Safety Stop

Plan Depth	Maximum Depth	Bottom Time	Time Out	Pressure Out

TIME

Wetsuit   **Drysuit**

Full / Shorty   Liner

_____ mm   Argon

Equipment

Weight _____ lb kg

Tank _____ cuft L

Pony tank _____ cuft L

- Camera
- Lighting
- Wreck reel
- Compass
- Knife
- Flashlight
- Spear gun
- Whistle
- Sausage
- Float N Flag
- Lift bag
- Float marker

Nitrox _____%
(for air use 21%)

MOD_____ft

Tri-Mix

O2 _____% N _____%

HE _____%

Rebreather Scrubber Monitor

Dive Scrubber_____ Minutes

Total Scrubber_____ Minutes

Dive partner:_____ PADI NAUI ACUC Other

Email/phone:_____ Cert. Number: _____

Sightings, Hazards, Notes, Photos, Sketches

DIVER'S LOG BOOK

Dive Number:	Date:

Location:
GPS:
Body of Water:
Site:

Dive Class

- Wreck
- Shore
- Reef
- River
- Ice
- Deep
- Cave
- Boat
- Certify
- Photo
- Video
- _____
- _____
- _____

Weather	☽	❄	☔	⛅	☀
Air Temp C/F	-10/14	0/32	10/50	20/68	30/86	40/104
Surface Temp	-10/14	0/32	10/50	20/68	30/86	40/104
Temp @ Depth	-10/14	0/32	10/50	20/68	30/86	40/104
Surface	Calm		Choppy		Waves
Current	None				Swift
Visibility M/ft	0	7.5/25	15/50	23/75	30/100

Dive Profile

- First Dive
- Second Dive
- Third Dive

DEPTH

Surface Interval	
Starting Group	
Time In		End Group
Pressure In		Safety Stop

Plan Depth	Maximum Depth	Bottom Time	Time Out	Pressure Out

TIME

Wetsuit	**Drysuit**	**Equipment**
Full / Shorty	Liner	Weight _____ lb kg
_____ mm	Argon	Tank _____ cuft L
		Pony tank _____ cuft L

- Camera
- Lighting
- Wreck reel
- Compass
- Knife
- Flashlight
- Spear gun
- Whistle
- Sausage
- Float N Flag
- Lift bag
- Float marker

Nitrox _____%
(for air use 21%)

MOD _____ ft

Tri-Mix

O2 _____% N _____%

HE _____%

Rebreather Scrubber Monitor

Dive Scrubber _____ Minutes

Total Scrubber _____ Minutes

Dive partner: _____   PADI   NAUI   ACUC   Other

Email/phone: _____   Cert. Number: _____

Sightings, Hazards, Notes, Photos, Sketches

Dive Number:		Date:
Location:		
GPS:		
Body of Water:		
Site:		

Dive Class

- Wreck
- Shore
- Reef
- River
- Ice
- Deep
- Cave
- Boat
- Certify
- Photo
- Video
- _____
- _____
- _____

Weather	☾	❄	🌧	⛅	☀
Air Temp C/F	-10/14	0/32	10/50	20/68	30/86	40/104
Surface Temp	-10/14	0/32	10/50	20/68	30/86	40/104
Temp @ Depth	-10/14	0/32	10/50	20/68	30/86	40/104
Surface	Calm		Choppy		Waves
Current	None				Swift
Visibility M/ft	0	7.5/25	15/50	23/75	30/100

Dive Profile

- First Dive
- Second Dive
- Third Dive

DEPTH

Surface Interval	
Starting Group	
Time In	End Group
Pressure In	Safety Stop

Plan Depth	Maximum Depth	Bottom Time	Time Out	Pressure Out

TIME

Wetsuit	**Drysuit**	**Equipment**	
Full / Shorty	Liner	Weight _____ lb kg	
_____ mm	Argon	Tank _____ cuft L	
		Pony tank _____ cuft L	

- Camera
- Lighting
- Wreck reel
- Compass
- Knife
- Flashlight
- Spear gun
- Whistle
- Sausage
- Float N Flag
- Lift bag
- Float marker

Nitrox _____ %
(for air use 21%)

MOD _____ ft

Tri-Mix

O2 _____ % N _____ %

HE _____ %

Rebreather Scrubber Monitor

Dive Scrubber _____ Minutes

Total Scrubber _____ Minutes

Dive partner: _____ PADI NAUI ACUC Other

Email/phone: _____ Cert. Number: _____

Sightings, Hazards, Notes, Photos, Sketches

DIVER'S LOG BOOK

	Dive Number:	Date:
	Location:	
	GPS:	
	Body of Water:	
	Site:	

Dive Class

- Wreck
- Boat
- Shore
- Certify
- Reef
- Photo
- River
- Video
- Ice
- _____
- Deep
- _____
- Cave
- _____

Weather	☾	☁❄	☔	⛅	☀
Air Temp C/F	-10/14	0/32	10/50	20/68	30/86	40/104
Surface Temp	-10/14	0/32	10/50	20/68	30/86	40/104
Temp @ Depth	-10/14	0/32	10/50	20/68	30/86	40/104
Surface	Calm		Choppy		Waves
Current	None				Swift
Visibility M/ft	0	7.5/25	15/50	23/75	30/100

Dive Profile

- First Dive
- Second Dive
- Third Dive

DEPTH

Surface Interval				
Starting Group				
Time In			End Group	
Pressure In			Safety Stop	
Plan Depth	Maximum Depth	Bottom Time	Time Out	Pressure Out

TIME

Wetsuit	**Drysuit**	**Equipment**			
Full / Shorty	Liner	Weight _____ lb kg	Camera	Knife	Sausage
_____ mm	Argon	Tank _____ cuft L	Lighting	Flashlight	Float N Flag
		Pony tank _____ cuft L	Wreck reel	Spear gun	Lift bag
			Compass	Whistle	Float marker

Nitrox _____ %
(for air use 21%)

MOD _____ ft

Tri-Mix

O2 ____ %   N ____ %

HE ____ %

Rebreather Scrubber Monitor

Dive Scrubber _____ Minutes

Total Scrubber _____ Minutes

Dive partner: _____ PADI NAUI ACUC Other

Email/phone: _____ Cert. Number: _____

Sightings, Hazards, Notes, Photos, Sketches

DIVER'S LOG BOOK

		Dive Number:		Date:	
		Location:			
		GPS:			
		Body of Water:			
		Site:			

Dive Class

- Wreck
- Shore
- Reef
- River
- Ice
- Deep
- Cave
- Boat
- Certify
- Photo
- Video
- _____
- _____
- _____

Weather	🌙	🌨	🌧	⛅	☀
Air Temp C/F	-10/14	0/32	10/50	20/68	30/86	40/104
Surface Temp	-10/14	0/32	10/50	20/68	30/86	40/104
Temp @ Depth	-10/14	0/32	10/50	20/68	30/86	40/104
Surface	Calm		Choppy			Waves
Current	None					Swift
Visibility M/ft	0	7.5/25	15/50	23/75	30/100

Dive Profile

- First Dive
- Second Dive
- Third Dive

DEPTH

Surface Interval				
Starting Group				
Time In			End Group	
Pressure In			Safety Stop	
Plan Depth	Maximum Depth	Bottom Time	Time Out	Pressure Out

TIME

Wetsuit	**Drysuit**	**Equipment**	Camera	Knife	Sausage
Full / Shorty	Liner	Weight _____ lb kg	Lighting	Flashlight	Float N Flag
____ mm	Argon	Tank _____ cuft L	Wreck reel	Spear gun	Lift bag
		Pony tank ____ cuft L	Compass	Whistle	Float marker

Nitrox _____% (for air use 21%) MOD _____ ft	**Tri-Mix** O2 ____% N ____% HE ____%	**Rebreather Scrubber Monitor** Dive Scrubber _____ Minutes Total Scrubber _____ Minutes

Dive partner: _____ PADI NAUI ACUC Other

Email/phone: _____ Cert. Number: _____

Sightings, Hazards, Notes, Photos, Sketches

DIVER'S LOG BOOK

Dive Number:	Date:

Location:

GPS:

Body of Water:

Site:

Dive Class

Weather	☾	☁❄	🌧	⛅	☀

- Wreck
- Shore
- Reef
- River
- Ice
- Deep
- Cave

- Boat
- Certify
- Photo
- Video
- _____
- _____
- _____

Air Temp C/F	-10/14	0/32	10/50	20/68	30/86	40/104
Surface Temp	-10/14	0/32	10/50	20/68	30/86	40/104
Temp @ Depth	-10/14	0/32	10/50	20/68	30/86	40/104
Surface	Calm		Choppy			Waves
Current	None					Swift
Visibility M/ft	0	7.5/25	15/50		23/75	30/100

Dive Profile   ● First Dive   ● Second Dive   ● Third Dive

D E P T H

Surface Interval	
Starting Group	
Time In	End Group
Pressure In	Safety Stop

Plan Depth	Maximum Depth	Bottom Time	Time Out	Pressure Out

TIME

Wetsuit	**Drysuit**	**Equipment**		
Full / Shorty	Liner	Weight _____lb kg		
_____ mm	Argon	Tank _____cuft L		
		Pony tank _____cuft L		

- Camera
- Lighting
- Wreck reel
- Compass

- Knife
- Flashlight
- Spear gun
- Whistle

- Sausage
- Float N Flag
- Lift bag
- Float marker

Nitrox _____%
(for air use 21%)

MOD_____ft

Tri-Mix

O2 ____% N ____%

HE ____%

Rebreather Scrubber Monitor

Dive Scrubber_____ Minutes

Total Scrubber_____ Minutes

Dive partner:_____ PADI NAUI ACUC Other

Email/phone:_____ Cert. Number: _____

Sightings, Hazards, Notes, Photos, Sketches

DIVER'S LOG BOOK

Dive Number:	Date:
Location:	
GPS:	
Body of Water:	
Site:	

Dive Class

- Wreck
- Shore
- Reef
- River
- Ice
- Deep
- Cave
- Boat
- Certify
- Photo
- Video
- _____
- _____
- _____

Weather	🌙	❄️	🌧️	⛅	☀️
Air Temp C/F	-10/14	0/32	10/50	20/68	30/86	40/104
Surface Temp	-10/14	0/32	10/50	20/68	30/86	40/104
Temp @ Depth	-10/14	0/32	10/50	20/68	30/86	40/104
Surface	Calm		Choppy		Waves
Current	None				Swift
Visibility M/ft	0	7.5/25	15/50	23/75	30/100

Dive Profile

- First Dive
- Second Dive
- Third Dive

DEPTH

Surface Interval		
Starting Group		
Time In		End Group
Pressure In		Safety Stop
Plan Depth	Maximum Depth	Bottom Time	Time Out	Pressure Out

TIME

Wetsuit	**Drysuit**	**Equipment**		
Full / Shorty	Liner	Weight _____ lb kg	Camera	Knife	Sausage
_____ mm	Argon	Tank _____ cuft L	Lighting	Flashlight	Float N Flag
		Pony tank _____ cuft L	Wreck reel	Spear gun	Lift bag
			Compass	Whistle	Float marker

Nitrox _____%
(for air use 21%)

MOD_____ft

Tri-Mix

O2 _____% N _____%

HE _____%

Rebreather Scrubber Monitor

Dive Scrubber_____ Minutes

Total Scrubber _____ Minutes

Dive partner:_____ PADI NAUI ACUC Other

Email/phone:_____ Cert. Number: _____

Sightings, Hazards, Notes, Photos, Sketches

	Dive Number:		Date:	
	Location:			
	GPS:			
	Body of Water:			
	Site:			

Dive Class

- Wreck
- Shore
- Reef
- River
- Ice
- Deep
- Cave

- Boat
- Certify
- Photo
- Video
- _____
- _____
- _____

Weather	☾	☁❄	☁☔	⛅	☀
Air Temp C/F	-10/14	0/32	10/50	20/68	30/86	40/104
Surface Temp	-10/14	0/32	10/50	20/68	30/86	40/104
Temp @ Depth	-10/14	0/32	10/50	20/68	30/86	40/104
Surface	Calm		Choppy		Waves
Current	None				Swift
Visibility M/ft	0	7.5/25	15/50	23/75	30/100

Dive Profile   ◯ First Dive   ◯ Second Dive   ◯ Third Dive

DEPTH

Surface Interval				
Starting Group				
Time In				End Group
Pressure In				Safety Stop
Plan Depth	Maximum Depth	Bottom Time	Time Out	Pressure Out

TIME

Wetsuit
Full / Shorty
_____ mm

Drysuit
Liner
Argon

Equipment
Weight _____ lb kg
Tank _____ cuft L
Pony tank _____ cuft L

- Camera
- Lighting
- Wreck reel
- Compass

- Knife
- Flashlight
- Spear gun
- Whistle

- Sausage
- Float N Flag
- Lift bag
- Float marker

Nitrox _____ %
(for air use 21%)

MOD_____ ft

Tri-Mix
O2 _____% N _____%
HE _____%

Rebreather Scrubber Monitor
Dive Scrubber_____ Minutes
Total Scrubber_____ Minutes

Dive partner:_____ PADI   NAUI   ACUC   Other

Email/phone:_____ Cert. Number: _____

Sightings, Hazards, Notes, Photos, Sketches

DIVER'S LOG BOOK

	Dive Number:	Date:
	Location:	
	GPS:	
	Body of Water:	
	Site:	

Dive Class

- ○ Wreck
- ○ Shore
- ○ Reef
- ○ River
- ○ Ice
- ○ Deep
- ○ Cave

- ○ Boat
- ○ Certify
- ○ Photo
- ○ Video
- ○ _____
- ○ _____
- ○ _____

Weather	☾	☁❄	☁☔	⛅	☀
Air Temp C/F	-10/14	0/32	10/50	20/68	30/86	40/104
Surface Temp	-10/14	0/32	10/50	20/68	30/86	40/104
Temp @ Depth	-10/14	0/32	10/50	20/68	30/86	40/104
Surface	Calm		Choppy		Waves
Current	None				Swift
Visibility M/ft	0	7.5/25	15/50	23/75	30/100

Dive Profile

○ First Dive ○ Second Dive ○ Third Dive

DEPTH

Surface Interval	
Starting Group	
Time In	End Group
Pressure In	Safety Stop

Plan Depth	Maximum Depth	Bottom Time	Time Out	Pressure Out

TIME

Wetsuit	**Drysuit**	**Equipment**
Full / Shorty	Liner	Weight _____ lb kg
_____ mm	Argon	Tank _____ cuft L
		Pony tank _____ cuft L

- ○ Camera
- ○ Lighting
- ○ Wreck reel
- ○ Compass

- ○ Knife
- ○ Flashlight
- ○ Spear gun
- ○ Whistle

- ○ Sausage
- ○ Float N Flag
- ○ Lift bag
- ○ Float marker

Nitrox _____% (for air use 21%)	**Tri-Mix**	**Rebreather Scrubber Monitor**
MOD_____ft	O2 ____% N ____%	Dive Scrubber_____ Minutes
	HE ____%	Total Scrubber _____ Minutes

Dive partner:_____ PADI NAUI ACUC Other

Email/phone:_____ Cert. Number: _____

Sightings, Hazards, Notes, Photos, Sketches

Dive Number:	Date:

Location:

GPS:

Body of Water:

Site:

Dive Class

- Wreck
- Shore
- Reef
- River
- Ice
- Deep
- Cave

- Boat
- Certify
- Photo
- Video
- _____
- _____
- _____

Weather	☾	❄	🌧	⛅	☀
Air Temp C/F	-10/14	0/32	10/50	20/68	30/86	40/104
Surface Temp	-10/14	0/32	10/50	20/68	30/86	40/104
Temp @ Depth	-10/14	0/32	10/50	20/68	30/86	40/104
Surface	Calm		Choppy		Waves
Current	None				Swift
Visibility M/ft	0	7.5/25	15/50	23/75	30/100

Dive Profile

○ First Dive   ○ Second Dive   ○ Third Dive

DEPTH

Surface Interval	
Starting Group	
Time In	End Group
Pressure In	Safety Stop

Plan Depth	Maximum Depth	Bottom Time	Time Out	Pressure Out

TIME

Wetsuit	**Drysuit**	**Equipment**
Full / Shorty	Liner	Weight _____ lb kg
_____ mm	Argon	Tank _____ cuft L
		Pony tank _____ cuft L

- ○ Camera
- ○ Lighting
- ○ Wreck reel
- ○ Compass

- ○ Knife
- ○ Flashlight
- ○ Spear gun
- ○ Whistle

- ○ Sausage
- ○ Float N Flag
- ○ Lift bag
- ○ Float marker

Nitrox _____ %
(for air use 21%)

MOD _____ ft

Tri-Mix

O2 ____ % N ____ %

HE ____ %

Rebreather Scrubber Monitor

Dive Scrubber _____ Minutes

Total Scrubber _____ Minutes

Dive partner: _____ PADI   NAUI   ACUC   Other

Email/phone: _____ Cert. Number: _____

Sightings, Hazards, Notes, Photos, Sketches

DIVER'S LOG BOOK

Dive Number:	Date:
Location:	
GPS:	
Body of Water:	
Site:	

Dive Class

- ⚪ Wreck
- ⚪ Shore
- ⚪ Reef
- ⚪ River
- ⚪ Ice
- ⚪ Deep
- ⚪ Cave
- ⚪ Boat
- ⚪ Certify
- ⚪ Photo
- ⚪ Video
- ⚪ _____
- ⚪ _____
- ⚪ _____

Weather	🌙	☁❄	🌧	⛅	☀
Air Temp C/F	-10/14	0/32	10/50	20/68	30/86	40/104
Surface Temp	-10/14	0/32	10/50	20/68	30/86	40/104
Temp @ Depth	-10/14	0/32	10/50	20/68	30/86	40/104
Surface	Calm		Choppy		Waves
Current	None				Swift
Visibility M/ft	0	7.5/25	15/50	23/75	30/100

Dive Profile   ⚪ First Dive   ⚪ Second Dive   ⚪ Third Dive

DEPTH

Surface Interval	
Starting Group	
Time In	End Group
Pressure In	Safety Stop

Plan Depth	Maximum Depth	Bottom Time	Time Out	Pressure Out

TIME

Wetsuit	**Drysuit**	**Equipment**	
Full / Shorty	Liner	Weight _____ lb kg	
_____ mm	Argon	Tank _____ cuft L	
		Pony tank _____ cuft L	

- ⚪ Camera
- ⚪ Lighting
- ⚪ Wreck reel
- ⚪ Compass
- ⚪ Knife
- ⚪ Flashlight
- ⚪ Spear gun
- ⚪ Whistle
- ⚪ Sausage
- ⚪ Float N Flag
- ⚪ Lift bag
- ⚪ Float marker

Nitrox _____ %
(for air use 21%)

MOD _____ ft

Tri-Mix

O2 ____ % N ____ %

HE ____ %

Rebreather Scrubber Monitor

Dive Scrubber _____ Minutes

Total Scrubber _____ Minutes

Dive partner: _____ PADI NAUI ACUC Other

Email/phone: _____ Cert. Number: _____

Sightings, Hazards, Notes, Photos, Sketches

	Dive Number:	Date:
	Location:	
	GPS:	
	Body of Water:	
	Site:	

Dive Class

- Wreck
- Shore
- Reef
- River
- Ice
- Deep
- Cave
- Boat
- Certify
- Photo
- Video
- _____
- _____
- _____

Weather	$\moon$	$\snow$	$\rain$	$\partlycloudy$	$\sun$
Air Temp C/F	-10/14	0/32	10/50	20/68	30/86	40/104
Surface Temp	-10/14	0/32	10/50	20/68	30/86	40/104
Temp @ Depth	-10/14	0/32	10/50	20/68	30/86	40/104
Surface	Calm		Choppy		Waves
Current	None				Swift
Visibility M/ft	0	7.5/25	15/50	23/75	30/100

Dive Profile

- First Dive
- Second Dive
- Third Dive

DEPTH

Surface Interval	
Starting Group	
Time In	End Group
Pressure In	Safety Stop

Plan Depth	Maximum Depth	Bottom Time	Time Out	Pressure Out

TIME

Wetsuit — Full / Shorty — _____ mm
Drysuit — Liner — Argon

Equipment
Weight _____ lb kg
Tank _____ cuft L
Pony tank _____ cuft L

- Camera
- Lighting
- Wreck reel
- Compass
- Knife
- Flashlight
- Spear gun
- Whistle
- Sausage
- Float N Flag
- Lift bag
- Float marker

Nitrox _____ %
(for air use 21%)

MOD _____ ft

Tri-Mix
O2 _____ % N _____ %
HE _____ %

Rebreather Scrubber Monitor
Dive Scrubber _____ Minutes
Total Scrubber _____ Minutes

Dive partner: _____ PADI NAUI ACUC Other

Email/phone: _____ Cert. Number: _____

Sightings, Hazards, Notes, Photos, Sketches

DIVER'S LOG BOOK

Dive Number:		Date:
Location:		
GPS:		
Body of Water:		
Site:		

Dive Class

- ○ Wreck
- ○ Shore
- ○ Reef
- ○ River
- ○ Ice
- ○ Deep
- ○ Cave
- ○ Boat
- ○ Certify
- ○ Photo
- ○ Video
- ○ _____
- ○ _____
- ○ _____

Weather	☾	❄	🌧	⛅	☀
Air Temp C/F	-10/14	0/32	10/50	20/68	30/86	40/104
Surface Temp	-10/14	0/32	10/50	20/68	30/86	40/104
Temp @ Depth	-10/14	0/32	10/50	20/68	30/86	40/104
Surface	Calm		Choppy		Waves
Current	None				Swift
Visibility M/ft	0	7.5/25	15/50	23/75	30/100

Dive Profile
○ First Dive ○ Second Dive ○ Third Dive

DEPTH

Surface Interval	
Starting Group	
Time In	End Group
Pressure In	Safety Stop
Plan Depth	Maximum Depth	Bottom Time	Time Out	Pressure Out

TIME

Wetsuit	Drysuit	Equipment			
Full / Shorty	Liner	Weight _____ lb kg	○ Camera	○ Knife	○ Sausage
_____ mm	Argon	Tank _____ cuft L	○ Lighting	○ Flashlight	○ Float N Flag
		Pony tank _____ cuft L	○ Wreck reel	○ Spear gun	○ Lift bag
			○ Compass	○ Whistle	○ Float marker

Nitrox _____ %	Tri-Mix	Rebreather Scrubber Monitor
(for air use 21%)	O2 _____% N _____%	Dive Scrubber _____ Minutes
MOD _____ ft	HE _____%	Total Scrubber _____ Minutes

Dive partner: _____ PADI NAUI ACUC Other

Email/phone: _____ Cert. Number: _____

Sightings, Hazards, Notes, Photos, Sketches

DIVER'S LOG BOOK

Dive Number:	Date:

Location:

GPS:

Body of Water:

Site:

Dive Class

- Wreck
- Shore
- Reef
- River
- Ice
- Deep
- Cave
- Boat
- Certify
- Photo
- Video
- _____
- _____
- _____

Weather	☽	❄	🌧	⛅	☀
Air Temp C/F	-10/14	0/32	10/50	20/68	30/86	40/104
Surface Temp	-10/14	0/32	10/50	20/68	30/86	40/104
Temp @ Depth	-10/14	0/32	10/50	20/68	30/86	40/104
Surface	Calm		Choppy		Waves
Current	None				Swift
Visibility M/ft	0	7.5/25	15/50	23/75	30/100

Dive Profile

- First Dive
- Second Dive
- Third Dive

D E P T H	Surface Interval			
	Starting Group			
	Time In		End Group	
	Pressure In		Safety Stop	
	Plan Depth	Maximum Depth	Bottom Time	Time Out	Pressure Out

TIME

Wetsuit	**Drysuit**
Full / Shorty	Liner
_____ mm	Argon

Equipment
Weight _____ lb kg
Tank _____ cuft L
Pony tank _____ cuft L

- Camera
- Lighting
- Wreck reel
- Compass
- Knife
- Flashlight
- Spear gun
- Whistle
- Sausage
- Float N Flag
- Lift bag
- Float marker

Nitrox _____ %
(for air use 21%)

MOD _____ ft

Tri-Mix
O2 ____ % N ____ %
HE ____ %

Rebreather Scrubber Monitor
Dive Scrubber _____ Minutes
Total Scrubber _____ Minutes

Dive partner: _____ PADI NAUI ACUC Other

Email/phone: _____ Cert. Number: _____

Sightings, Hazards, Notes, Photos, Sketches

DIVER'S LOG BOOK

Dive Number:		Date:
Location:		
GPS:		
Body of Water:		
Site:		

Dive Class

- Wreck
- Shore
- Reef
- River
- Ice
- Deep
- Cave
- Boat
- Certify
- Photo
- Video
- _____
- _____
- _____

Weather	☾	❄	🌧	⛅	☀
Air Temp C/F	-10/14	0/32	10/50	20/68	30/86	40/104
Surface Temp	-10/14	0/32	10/50	20/68	30/86	40/104
Temp @ Depth	-10/14	0/32	10/50	20/68	30/86	40/104
Surface	Calm		Choppy		Waves
Current	None				Swift
Visibility M/ft	0	7.5/25	15/50	23/75	30/100

Dive Profile

- First Dive
- Second Dive
- Third Dive

D E P T H

Surface Interval				
Starting Group				
Time In				End Group
Pressure In				Safety Stop
Plan Depth	Maximum Depth	Bottom Time	Time Out	Pressure Out

TIME

Wetsuit	**Drysuit**	**Equipment**	
Full / Shorty	Liner	Weight _____ lb kg	
_____ mm	Argon	Tank _____ cuft L	
		Pony tank _____ cuft L	

- Camera
- Lighting
- Wreck reel
- Compass
- Knife
- Flashlight
- Spear gun
- Whistle
- Sausage
- Float N Flag
- Lift bag
- Float marker

Nitrox _____ % (for air use 21%) MOD _____ ft	**Tri-Mix** O2 _____% N _____% HE _____%	**Rebreather Scrubber Monitor** Dive Scrubber _____ Minutes Total Scrubber _____ Minutes

Dive partner: _____ PADI NAUI ACUC Other

Email/phone: _____ Cert. Number: _____

Sightings, Hazards, Notes, Photos, Sketches

DIVER'S LOG BOOK

Dive Number:	Date:
Location:	
GPS:	
Body of Water:	
Site:	

Dive Class

- Wreck
- Shore
- Reef
- River
- Ice
- Deep
- Cave
- Boat
- Certify
- Photo
- Video
- _____
- _____
- _____

Weather	🌙	☁❄	🌧	⛅	☀
Air Temp C/F	-10/14	0/32	10/50	20/68	30/86	40/104
Surface Temp	-10/14	0/32	10/50	20/68	30/86	40/104
Temp @ Depth	-10/14	0/32	10/50	20/68	30/86	40/104
Surface	Calm		Choppy			Waves
Current	None					Swift
Visibility M/ft	0	7.5/25		15/50	23/75	30/100

Dive Profile

- First Dive
- Second Dive
- Third Dive

DEPTH

Surface Interval	
Starting Group	
Time In	End Group
Pressure In	Safety Stop

Plan Depth	Maximum Depth	Bottom Time	Time Out	Pressure Out

TIME

Wetsuit **Drysuit**

Full / Shorty   Liner

_____ mm   Argon

Equipment

Weight _____ lb kg

Tank _____ cuft L

Pony tank _____ cuft L

- Camera
- Lighting
- Wreck reel
- Compass
- Knife
- Flashlight
- Spear gun
- Whistle
- Sausage
- Float N Flag
- Lift bag
- Float marker

Nitrox _____%
(for air use 21%)

MOD _____ ft

Tri-Mix

O2 _____% N _____%

HE _____%

Rebreather Scrubber Monitor

Dive Scrubber _____ Minutes

Total Scrubber _____ Minutes

Dive partner: _____ PADI NAUI ACUC Other

Email/phone: _____ Cert. Number: _____

Sightings, Hazards, Notes, Photos, Sketches

DIVER'S LOG BOOK

Dive Number:		Date:
Location:		
GPS:		
Body of Water:		
Site:		

Dive Class

○ Wreck	○ Boat
○ Shore	○ Certify
○ Reef	○ Photo
○ River	○ Video
○ Ice	○ _____
○ Deep	○ _____
○ Cave	○ _____

Weather	☾	☁❄	☁☔	⛅	☀
Air Temp C/F	-10/14	0/32	10/50	20/68	30/86	40/104
Surface Temp	-10/14	0/32	10/50	20/68	30/86	40/104
Temp @ Depth	-10/14	0/32	10/50	20/68	30/86	40/104
Surface	Calm		Choppy		Waves
Current	None				Swift
Visibility M/ft	0	7.5/25	15/50	23/75	30/100

Dive Profile   ○ First Dive   ○ Second Dive   ○ Third Dive

D E P T H	Surface Interval			
	Starting Group			
	Time In			End Group
	Pressure In			Safety Stop
	Plan Depth	Maximum Depth	Bottom Time	Time Out	Pressure Out

TIME

Wetsuit	**Drysuit**	**Equipment**		
Full / Shorty	Liner	Weight _____ lb kg	○ Camera	○ Knife	○ Sausage
_____ mm	Argon	Tank _____ cuft L	○ Lighting	○ Flashlight	○ Float N Flag
		Pony tank _____ cuft L	○ Wreck reel	○ Spear gun	○ Lift bag
			○ Compass	○ Whistle	○ Float marker

Nitrox _____ % (for air use 21%)	**Tri-Mix**	**Rebreather Scrubber Monitor**
	O2 _____ % N _____ %	Dive Scrubber _____ Minutes
MOD _____ ft	HE _____ %	Total Scrubber _____ Minutes

Dive partner: _____ PADI NAUI ACUC Other

Email/phone: _____ Cert. Number: _____

Sightings, Hazards, Notes, Photos, Sketches

DIVER'S LOG BOOK

Dive Number:	Date:
Location:	
GPS:	
Body of Water:	
Site:	

Dive Class

- ○ Wreck
- ○ Shore
- ○ Reef
- ○ River
- ○ Ice
- ○ Deep
- ○ Cave
- ○ Boat
- ○ Certify
- ○ Photo
- ○ Video
- ○ _____
- ○ _____
- ○ _____

Weather	☽	❄	🌧	⛅	☀
Air Temp C/F	-10/14	0/32	10/50	20/68	30/86	40/104
Surface Temp	-10/14	0/32	10/50	20/68	30/86	40/104
Temp @ Depth	-10/14	0/32	10/50	20/68	30/86	40/104
Surface	Calm		Choppy			Waves
Current	None					Swift
Visibility M/ft	0	7.5/25		15/50	23/75	30/100

Dive Profile   ○ First Dive   ○ Second Dive   ○ Third Dive

D E P T H

Surface Interval	
Starting Group	
Time In	End Group
Pressure In	Safety Stop

Plan Depth	Maximum Depth	Bottom Time	Time Out	Pressure Out

TIME

Wetsuit	**Drysuit**	**Equipment**		
Full / Shorty	Liner	Weight _____ lb kg	○ Camera	○ Knife	○ Sausage
_____ mm	Argon	Tank _____ cuft L	○ Lighting	○ Flashlight	○ Float N Flag
		Pony tank _____ cuft L	○ Wreck reel	○ Spear gun	○ Lift bag
			○ Compass	○ Whistle	○ Float marker

Nitrox _____ %
(for air use 21%)

MOD _____ ft

Tri-Mix

O2 _____ %   N _____ %

HE _____ %

Rebreather Scrubber Monitor

Dive Scrubber _____ Minutes

Total Scrubber _____ Minutes

Dive partner: _____ PADI NAUI ACUC Other

Email/phone: _____ Cert. Number: _____

Sightings, Hazards, Notes, Photos, Sketches

		Dive Number:	Date:
		Location:	
		GPS:	
		Body of Water:	
		Site:	

Dive Class

- Wreck
- Boat
- Shore
- Certify
- Reef
- Photo
- River
- Video
- Ice
- _____
- Deep
- _____
- Cave
- _____

Weather	☾	❄	🌧	⛅	☀
Air Temp C/F	-10/14	0/32	10/50	20/68	30/86	40/104
Surface Temp	-10/14	0/32	10/50	20/68	30/86	40/104
Temp @ Depth	-10/14	0/32	10/50	20/68	30/86	40/104
Surface	Calm		Choppy		Waves
Current	None				Swift
Visibility M/ft	0	7.5/25	15/50	23/75	30/100

Dive Profile

- First Dive
- Second Dive
- Third Dive

DEPTH

Surface Interval	
Starting Group	
Time In	End Group
Pressure In	Safety Stop

Plan Depth	Maximum Depth	Bottom Time	Time Out	Pressure Out

TIME

Wetsuit	**Drysuit**	**Equipment**		
Full / Shorty	Liner	Weight _____ lb kg	Camera	Knife	Sausage
_____ mm	Argon	Tank _____ cuft L	Lighting	Flashlight	Float N Flag
		Pony tank _____ cuft L	Wreck reel	Spear gun	Lift bag
			Compass	Whistle	Float marker

Nitrox _____ % (for air use 21%)	**Tri-Mix**	**Rebreather Scrubber Monitor**
	O2 ____ % N ____ %	Dive Scrubber _____ Minutes
MOD _____ ft	HE ____ %	Total Scrubber _____ Minutes

Dive partner: _____ PADI NAUI ACUC Other

Email/phone: _____ Cert. Number: _____

Sightings, Hazards, Notes, Photos, Sketches

Dive Number:	Date:

Location:
GPS:
Body of Water:
Site:

Dive Class

- Wreck
- Shore
- Reef
- River
- Ice
- Deep
- Cave
- Boat
- Certify
- Photo
- Video
- _____
- _____
- _____

Weather	☾	❄	☔	⛅	☀
Air Temp C/F	-10/14	0/32	10/50	20/68	30/86	40/104
Surface Temp	-10/14	0/32	10/50	20/68	30/86	40/104
Temp @ Depth	-10/14	0/32	10/50	20/68	30/86	40/104
Surface	Calm		Choppy		Waves
Current	None				Swift
Visibility M/ft	0	7.5/25	15/50	23/75	30/100

Dive Profile

- First Dive
- Second Dive
- Third Dive

DEPTH

Surface Interval	
Starting Group	
Time In	End Group
Pressure In	Safety Stop
Plan Depth	Maximum Depth	Bottom Time	Time Out	Pressure Out

TIME

Wetsuit	Drysuit	Equipment
Full / Shorty	Liner	Weight _____ lb kg
_____ mm	Argon	Tank _____ cuft L
		Pony tank _____ cuft L

- Camera
- Lighting
- Wreck reel
- Compass
- Knife
- Flashlight
- Spear gun
- Whistle
- Sausage
- Float N Flag
- Lift bag
- Float marker

Nitrox _____%
(for air use 21%)

MOD _____ ft

Tri-Mix

O2 _____% N _____%

HE _____%

Rebreather Scrubber Monitor

Dive Scrubber _____ Minutes

Total Scrubber _____ Minutes

Dive partner: _____ PADI NAUI ACUC Other

Email/phone: _____ Cert. Number: _____

Sightings, Hazards, Notes, Photos, Sketches

Dive Number:		Date:	
Location:			
GPS:			
Body of Water:			
Site:			

Dive Class

- Wreck
- Shore
- Reef
- River
- Ice
- Deep
- Cave
- Boat
- Certify
- Photo
- Video
- _____
- _____
- _____

Weather	🌙	❄	🌧	⛅	☀
Air Temp C/F	-10/14	0/32	10/50	20/68	30/86	40/104
Surface Temp	-10/14	0/32	10/50	20/68	30/86	40/104
Temp @ Depth	-10/14	0/32	10/50	20/68	30/86	40/104
Surface	Calm		Choppy		Waves
Current	None				Swift
Visibility M/ft	0	7.5/25	15/50	23/75	30/100

Dive Profile

- First Dive
- Second Dive
- Third Dive

DEPTH

Surface Interval				
Starting Group				
Time In				End Group
Pressure In				Safety Stop
Plan Depth	Maximum Depth	Bottom Time	Time Out	Pressure Out

TIME

Wetsuit
Full / Shorty
____ mm

Drysuit
Liner
Argon

Equipment
Weight _____ lb kg
Tank _____ cuft L
Pony tank _____ cuft L

- Camera
- Lighting
- Wreck reel
- Compass
- Knife
- Flashlight
- Spear gun
- Whistle
- Sausage
- Float N Flag
- Lift bag
- Float marker

Nitrox _____ %
(for air use 21%)
MOD _____ ft

Tri-Mix
O2 ____ % N ____ %
HE ____ %

Rebreather Scrubber Monitor
Dive Scrubber _____ Minutes
Total Scrubber _____ Minutes

Dive partner: _____ PADI NAUI ACUC Other

Email/phone: _____ Cert. Number: _____

Sightings, Hazards, Notes, Photos, Sketches

DIVER'S LOG BOOK

	Dive Number:	Date:
	Location:	
	GPS:	
	Body of Water:	
	Site:	

Dive Class

- Wreck
- Shore
- Reef
- River
- Ice
- Deep
- Cave
- Boat
- Certify
- Photo
- Video
- _____
- _____
- _____

Weather	☾	❄	☔	⛅	☀
Air Temp C/F	-10/14	0/32	10/50	20/68	30/86	40/104
Surface Temp	-10/14	0/32	10/50	20/68	30/86	40/104
Temp @ Depth	-10/14	0/32	10/50	20/68	30/86	40/104
Surface	Calm		Choppy		Waves
Current	None				Swift
Visibility M/ft	0	7.5/25	15/50	23/75	30/100

Dive Profile

- First Dive
- Second Dive
- Third Dive

DEPTH

Surface Interval	
Starting Group	
Time In	End Group
Pressure In	Safety Stop

Plan Depth	Maximum Depth	Bottom Time	Time Out	Pressure Out

TIME

Wetsuit
Full / Shorty
_____ mm

Drysuit
Liner
Argon

Equipment
Weight _____ lb kg
Tank _____ cuft L
Pony tank _____ cuft L

- Camera
- Lighting
- Wreck reel
- Compass
- Knife
- Flashlight
- Spear gun
- Whistle
- Sausage
- Float N Flag
- Lift bag
- Float marker

Nitrox _____ %
(for air use 21%)

MOD _____ ft

Tri-Mix
O2 _____ % N _____ %
HE _____ %

Rebreather Scrubber Monitor
Dive Scrubber _____ Minutes
Total Scrubber _____ Minutes

Dive partner: _____ PADI NAUI ACUC Other

Email/phone: _____ Cert. Number: _____

Sightings, Hazards, Notes, Photos, Sketches

DIVER'S LOG BOOK

	Dive Number:	Date:
	Location:	
	GPS:	
	Body of Water:	
	Site:	

Dive Class

- ○ Wreck
- ○ Boat
- ○ Shore
- ○ Certify
- ○ Reef
- ○ Photo
- ○ River
- ○ Video
- ○ Ice
- ○ _____
- ○ Deep
- ○ _____
- ○ Cave
- ○ _____

Weather	☾	☁❄	☁☂	⛅	☀
Air Temp C/F	-10/14	0/32	10/50	20/68	30/86	40/104
Surface Temp	-10/14	0/32	10/50	20/68	30/86	40/104
Temp @ Depth	-10/14	0/32	10/50	20/68	30/86	40/104
Surface	Calm		Choppy		Waves
Current	None				Swift
Visibility M/ft	0	7.5/25	15/50	23/75	30/100

Dive Profile   ○ First Dive   ○ Second Dive   ○ Third Dive

D E P T H	Surface Interval				
	Starting Group				
	Time In				End Group
	Pressure In				Safety Stop
	Plan Depth	Maximum Depth	Bottom Time	Time Out	Pressure Out

TIME

Wetsuit	**Drysuit**	**Equipment**		
Full / Shorty	Liner	Weight _____ lb kg	○ Camera	○ Knife	○ Sausage
_____ mm	Argon	Tank _____ cuft L	○ Lighting	○ Flashlight	○ Float N Flag
		Pony tank _____ cuft L	○ Wreck reel	○ Spear gun	○ Lift bag
			○ Compass	○ Whistle	○ Float marker

Nitrox _____ % (for air use 21%) MOD _____ ft	**Tri-Mix** O2 _____ % N _____ % HE _____ %	**Rebreather Scrubber Monitor** Dive Scrubber _____ Minutes Total Scrubber _____ Minutes

Dive partner: _____   PADI NAUI ACUC Other

Email/phone: _____   Cert. Number: _____

Sightings, Hazards, Notes, Photos, Sketches

	Dive Number:	Date:
	Location:	
	GPS:	
	Body of Water:	
	Site:	

Dive Class

- ○ Wreck
- ○ Boat
- ○ Shore
- ○ Certify
- ○ Reef
- ○ Photo
- ○ River
- ○ Video
- ○ Ice
- ○ _____
- ○ Deep
- ○ _____
- ○ Cave
- ○ _____

Weather	☽	❄	☔	☁	☀
Air Temp C/F	-10/14	0/32	10/50	20/68	30/86	40/104
Surface Temp	-10/14	0/32	10/50	20/68	30/86	40/104
Temp @ Depth	-10/14	0/32	10/50	20/68	30/86	40/104
Surface	Calm		Choppy		Waves
Current	None				Swift
Visibility M/ft	0	7.5/25	15/50	23/75	30/100

Dive Profile
○ First Dive ○ Second Dive ○ Third Dive

DEPTH

Surface Interval		
Starting Group		
Time In		End Group
Pressure In		Safety Stop
Plan Depth	Maximum Depth	Bottom Time	Time Out	Pressure Out

TIME

Wetsuit **Drysuit**
Full / Shorty   Liner
_____ mm   Argon

Equipment
Weight _____ lb kg
Tank _____ cuft L
Pony tank _____ cuft L

- ○ Camera
- ○ Knife
- ○ Sausage
- ○ Lighting
- ○ Flashlight
- ○ Float N Flag
- ○ Wreck reel
- ○ Spear gun
- ○ Lift bag
- ○ Compass
- ○ Whistle
- ○ Float marker

Nitrox _____ %
(for air use 21%)

MOD _____ ft

Tri-Mix
O2 _____ % N _____ %
HE _____ %

Rebreather Scrubber Monitor
Dive Scrubber _____ Minutes
Total Scrubber _____ Minutes

Dive partner: _____ PADI NAUI ACUC Other

Email/phone: _____ Cert. Number: _____

Sightings, Hazards, Notes, Photos, Sketches

Dive Number:	Date:
Location:	
GPS:	
Body of Water:	
Site:	

Dive Class

- Wreck
- Shore
- Reef
- River
- Ice
- Deep
- Cave
- Boat
- Certify
- Photo
- Video
- _____
- _____
- _____

Weather	☽	☁❄	🌧	⛅	☀
Air Temp C/F	-10/14	0/32	10/50	20/68	30/86	40/104
Surface Temp	-10/14	0/32	10/50	20/68	30/86	40/104
Temp @ Depth	-10/14	0/32	10/50	20/68	30/86	40/104
Surface	Calm		Choppy		Waves
Current	None				Swift
Visibility M/ft	0	7.5/25	15/50	23/75	30/100

Dive Profile   ⦿ First Dive   ⦿ Second Dive   ⦿ Third Dive

DEPTH

Surface Interval	
Starting Group	
Time In	End Group
Pressure In	Safety Stop

Plan Depth	Maximum Depth	Bottom Time	Time Out	Pressure Out

TIME

Wetsuit	**Drysuit**	**Equipment**		
Full / Shorty	Liner	Weight _____ lb kg		
_____ mm	Argon	Tank _____ cuft L		
		Pony tank _____ cuft L		

- Camera
- Lighting
- Wreck reel
- Compass
- Knife
- Flashlight
- Spear gun
- Whistle
- Sausage
- Float N Flag
- Lift bag
- Float marker

Nitrox _____%
(for air use 21%)

MOD_____ft

Tri-Mix

O2 ____% N ____%

HE ____%

Rebreather Scrubber Monitor

Dive Scrubber_____ Minutes

Total Scrubber_____ Minutes

Dive partner:_____ PADI NAUI ACUC Other

Email/phone:_____ Cert. Number: _____

Sightings, Hazards, Notes, Photos, Sketches

Dive Number:	Date:
Location:	
GPS:	
Body of Water:	
Site:	

Dive Class

- ◯ Wreck
- ◯ Boat
- ◯ Shore
- ◯ Certify
- ◯ Reef
- ◯ Photo
- ◯ River
- ◯ Video
- ◯ Ice
- ◯ _____
- ◯ Deep
- ◯ _____
- ◯ Cave
- ◯ _____

Weather	☾	☁❄	☁🌧	⛅	☀
Air Temp C/F	-10/14	0/32	10/50	20/68	30/86	40/104
Surface Temp	-10/14	0/32	10/50	20/68	30/86	40/104
Temp @ Depth	-10/14	0/32	10/50	20/68	30/86	40/104
Surface	Calm		Choppy		Waves
Current	None				Swift
Visibility M/ft	0	7.5/25	15/50	23/75	30/100

Dive Profile ◯ First Dive ◯ Second Dive ◯ Third Dive

DEPTH

Surface Interval	
Starting Group	
Time In	End Group
Pressure In	Safety Stop

Plan Depth	Maximum Depth	Bottom Time	Time Out	Pressure Out

TIME

Wetsuit	**Drysuit**	**Equipment**	
Full / Shorty	Liner	Weight _____ lb kg	
_____ mm	Argon	Tank _____ cuft L	
		Pony tank _____ cuft L	

- ◯ Camera
- ◯ Knife
- ◯ Sausage
- ◯ Lighting
- ◯ Flashlight
- ◯ Float N Flag
- ◯ Wreck reel
- ◯ Spear gun
- ◯ Lift bag
- ◯ Compass
- ◯ Whistle
- ◯ Float marker

Nitrox _____ % (for air use 21%)	**Tri-Mix**	**Rebreather Scrubber Monitor**
MOD _____ ft	O2 ____% N ____%	Dive Scrubber _____ Minutes
	HE ____%	Total Scrubber _____ Minutes

Dive partner: _____ PADI NAUI ACUC Other

Email/phone: _____ Cert. Number: _____

Sightings, Hazards, Notes, Photos, Sketches

DIVER'S LOG BOOK

		Dive Number:	Date:
		Location:	
		GPS:	
		Body of Water:	
		Site:	

Dive Class

- Wreck
- Shore
- Reef
- River
- Ice
- Deep
- Cave
- Boat
- Certify
- Photo
- Video
- _____
- _____
- _____

Weather	🌙	☁️❄️	🌧️	⛅	☀️
Air Temp C/F	-10/14	0/32	10/50	20/68	30/86	40/104
Surface Temp	-10/14	0/32	10/50	20/68	30/86	40/104
Temp @ Depth	-10/14	0/32	10/50	20/68	30/86	40/104
Surface	Calm		Choppy		Waves
Current	None				Swift
Visibility M/ft	0	7.5/25	15/50	23/75	30/100

Dive Profile

○ First Dive ○ Second Dive ○ Third Dive

DEPTH

Surface Interval				
Starting Group				
Time In			End Group	
Pressure In			Safety Stop	
Plan Depth	Maximum Depth	Bottom Time	Time Out	Pressure Out

TIME

Wetsuit	**Drysuit**	**Equipment**
Full / Shorty	Liner	Weight _____ lb kg
_____ mm	Argon	Tank _____ cuft L
		Pony tank _____ cuft L

- Camera
- Lighting
- Wreck reel
- Compass
- Knife
- Flashlight
- Spear gun
- Whistle
- Sausage
- Float N Flag
- Lift bag
- Float marker

Nitrox _____ %
(for air use 21%)

MOD _____ ft

Tri-Mix

O2 _____ % N _____ %

HE _____ %

Rebreather Scrubber Monitor

Dive Scrubber _____ Minutes

Total Scrubber _____ Minutes

Dive partner: _____ PADI NAUI ACUC Other

Email/phone: _____ Cert. Number: _____

Sightings, Hazards, Notes, Photos, Sketches

DIVER'S LOG BOOK

Dive Number:		Date:
Location:		
GPS:		
Body of Water:		
Site:		

Dive Class

- Wreck
- Boat
- Shore
- Certify
- Reef
- Photo
- River
- Video
- Ice
- _____
- Deep
- _____
- Cave
- _____

Weather	☾	☁❄	🌧	⛅	☀
Air Temp C/F	-10/14	0/32	10/50	20/68	30/86	40/104
Surface Temp	-10/14	0/32	10/50	20/68	30/86	40/104
Temp @ Depth	-10/14	0/32	10/50	20/68	30/86	40/104
Surface	Calm		Choppy		Waves
Current	None				Swift
Visibility M/ft	0	7.5/25	15/50	23/75	30/100

Dive Profile

- First Dive
- Second Dive
- Third Dive

DEPTH	Surface Interval	
	Starting Group	
	Time In	End Group
	Pressure In	Safety Stop

Plan Depth	Maximum Depth	Bottom Time	Time Out	Pressure Out

TIME

Wetsuit	**Drysuit**	**Equipment**		
Full / Shorty	Liner	Weight _____ lb kg		
_____ mm	Argon	Tank _____ cuft L		
		Pony tank _____ cuft L		

- Camera
- Knife
- Sausage
- Lighting
- Flashlight
- Float N Flag
- Wreck reel
- Spear gun
- Lift bag
- Compass
- Whistle
- Float marker

Nitrox _____% (for air use 21%)	**Tri-Mix**	**Rebreather Scrubber Monitor**
	O2 ____% N ____%	Dive Scrubber _____ Minutes
MOD _____ ft	HE ____%	Total Scrubber _____ Minutes

Dive partner: _____ PADI NAUI ACUC Other

Email/phone: _____ Cert. Number: _____

Sightings, Hazards, Notes, Photos, Sketches

DIVER'S LOG BOOK

Dive Number:	Date:
Location:	
GPS:	
Body of Water:	
Site:	

Dive Class

- ○ Wreck
- ○ Shore
- ○ Reef
- ○ River
- ○ Ice
- ○ Deep
- ○ Cave
- ○ Boat
- ○ Certify
- ○ Photo
- ○ Video
- ○ _____
- ○ _____
- ○ _____

Weather	🌙	❄️	🌧️	⛅	☀️
Air Temp C/F	-10/14	0/32	10/50	20/68	30/86	40/104
Surface Temp	-10/14	0/32	10/50	20/68	30/86	40/104
Temp @ Depth	-10/14	0/32	10/50	20/68	30/86	40/104
Surface	Calm		Choppy		Waves
Current	None				Swift
Visibility M/ft	0	7.5/25	15/50	23/75	30/100

Dive Profile

○ First Dive ○ Second Dive ○ Third Dive

DEPTH

Surface Interval	
Starting Group	
Time In	End Group
Pressure In	Safety Stop

Plan Depth	Maximum Depth	Bottom Time	Time Out	Pressure Out

TIME

Wetsuit	Drysuit	Equipment
Full / Shorty	Liner	Weight _____ lb kg
_____ mm	Argon	Tank _____ cuft L
		Pony tank _____ cuft L

- ○ Camera
- ○ Lighting
- ○ Wreck reel
- ○ Compass
- ○ Knife
- ○ Flashlight
- ○ Spear gun
- ○ Whistle
- ○ Sausage
- ○ Float N Flag
- ○ Lift bag
- ○ Float marker

Nitrox _____ %
(for air use 21%)

MOD _____ ft

Tri-Mix

O2 _____ % N _____ %

HE _____ %

Rebreather Scrubber Monitor

Dive Scrubber _____ Minutes

Total Scrubber _____ Minutes

Dive partner: _____ PADI NAUI ACUC Other

Email/phone: _____ Cert. Number: _____

Sightings, Hazards, Notes, Photos, Sketches

DIVER'S LOG BOOK

Dive Number:	Date:

Location:
GPS:
Body of Water:
Site:

Dive Class

- Wreck
- Shore
- Reef
- River
- Ice
- Deep
- Cave
- Boat
- Certify
- Photo
- Video
- _____
- _____
- _____

Weather	☾	☁❄	🌧	⛅	☀
Air Temp C/F	-10/14	0/32	10/50	20/68	30/86	40/104
Surface Temp	-10/14	0/32	10/50	20/68	30/86	40/104
Temp @ Depth	-10/14	0/32	10/50	20/68	30/86	40/104
Surface	Calm		Choppy		Waves
Current	None				Swift
Visibility M/ft	0	7.5/25	15/50	23/75	30/100

Dive Profile

- First Dive
- Second Dive
- Third Dive

DEPTH

Surface Interval				
Starting Group				
Time In				End Group
Pressure In				Safety Stop
Plan Depth	Maximum Depth	Bottom Time	Time Out	Pressure Out

TIME

Wetsuit	**Drysuit**	**Equipment**
Full / Shorty	Liner	Weight _____ lb kg
_____ mm	Argon	Tank _____ cuft L
		Pony tank _____ cuft L

- Camera
- Lighting
- Wreck reel
- Compass
- Knife
- Flashlight
- Spear gun
- Whistle
- Sausage
- Float N Flag
- Lift bag
- Float marker

Nitrox _____%
(for air use 21%)

MOD_____ft

Tri-Mix

O2 _____% N _____%

HE _____%

Rebreather Scrubber Monitor

Dive Scrubber _____ Minutes

Total Scrubber _____ Minutes

Dive partner: _____ PADI NAUI ACUC Other

Email/phone: _____ Cert. Number: _____

Sightings, Hazards, Notes, Photos, Sketches

DIVER'S LOG BOOK

	Dive Number:	Date:
	Location:	
	GPS:	
	Body of Water:	
	Site:	

Dive Class

- ⚪ Wreck
- ⚪ Shore
- ⚪ Reef
- ⚪ River
- ⚪ Ice
- ⚪ Deep
- ⚪ Cave
- ⚪ Boat
- ⚪ Certify
- ⚪ Photo
- ⚪ Video
- ⚪ _____
- ⚪ _____
- ⚪ _____

Weather	☾	❄	🌧	⛅	☀
Air Temp C/F	-10/14	0/32	10/50	20/68	30/86	40/104
Surface Temp	-10/14	0/32	10/50	20/68	30/86	40/104
Temp @ Depth	-10/14	0/32	10/50	20/68	30/86	40/104
Surface	Calm		Choppy		Waves
Current	None				Swift
Visibility M/ft	0	7.5/25	15/50	23/75	30/100

Dive Profile

⚪ First Dive   ⚪ Second Dive   ⚪ Third Dive

DEPTH

Surface Interval	
Starting Group	
Time In		End Group
Pressure In		Safety Stop
Plan Depth	Maximum Depth	Bottom Time	Time Out	Pressure Out

TIME

Wetsuit	**Drysuit**	**Equipment**		
Full / Shorty	Liner	Weight _____ lb kg	⚪ Camera	⚪ Knife	⚪ Sausage
_____ mm	Argon	Tank _____ cuft L	⚪ Lighting	⚪ Flashlight	⚪ Float N Flag
		Pony tank _____ cuft L	⚪ Wreck reel	⚪ Spear gun	⚪ Lift bag
			⚪ Compass	⚪ Whistle	⚪ Float marker

Nitrox _____ % (for air use 21%) MOD _____ ft	**Tri-Mix** O2 ____ % N ____ % HE ____ %	**Rebreather Scrubber Monitor** Dive Scrubber _____ Minutes Total Scrubber _____ Minutes

Dive partner: _____ PADI NAUI ACUC Other

Email/phone: _____ Cert. Number: _____

Sightings, Hazards, Notes, Photos, Sketches

DIVER'S LOG BOOK

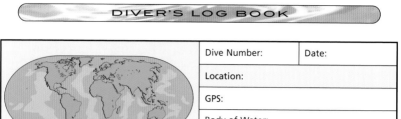

	Dive Number:	Date:
	Location:	
	GPS:	
	Body of Water:	
	Site:	

Dive Class

- ○ Wreck
- ○ Boat
- ○ Shore
- ○ Certify
- ○ Reef
- ○ Photo
- ○ River
- ○ Video
- ○ Ice
- ○ _____
- ○ Deep
- ○ _____
- ○ Cave
- ○ _____

Weather	☾	❄☁	☁🌧	⛅	☀
Air Temp C/F	-10/14	0/32	10/50	20/68	30/86	40/104
Surface Temp	-10/14	0/32	10/50	20/68	30/86	40/104
Temp @ Depth	-10/14	0/32	10/50	20/68	30/86	40/104
Surface	Calm		Choppy		Waves
Current	None				Swift
Visibility M/ft	0	7.5/25	15/50	23/75	30/100

Dive Profile

○ First Dive   ○ Second Dive   ○ Third Dive

D E P T H

Surface Interval	
Starting Group	
Time In	End Group
Pressure In	Safety Stop

Plan Depth	Maximum Depth	Bottom Time	Time Out	Pressure Out

TIME

Wetsuit	**Drysuit**
Full / Shorty	Liner
_____ mm	Argon

Equipment

Weight _____ lb kg
Tank _____ cuft L
Pony tank _____ cuft L

- ○ Camera
- ○ Knife
- ○ Sausage
- ○ Lighting
- ○ Flashlight
- ○ Float N Flag
- ○ Wreck reel
- ○ Spear gun
- ○ Lift bag
- ○ Compass
- ○ Whistle
- ○ Float marker

Nitrox _____%
(for air use 21%)

MOD_____ft

Tri-Mix

O2 ____% N ____%

HE ____%

Rebreather Scrubber Monitor

Dive Scrubber_____ Minutes

Total Scrubber_____ Minutes

Dive partner:_____ PADI NAUI ACUC Other

Email/phone:_____ Cert. Number: _____

Sightings, Hazards, Notes, Photos, Sketches

DIVER'S LOG BOOK

	Dive Number:	Date:

Location:
GPS:
Body of Water:
Site:

Dive Class

- Wreck
- Shore
- Reef
- River
- Ice
- Deep
- Cave
- Boat
- Certify
- Photo
- Video
- _____
- _____
- _____

Weather	🌙	❄️	🌧️	⛅	☀️
Air Temp C/F	-10/14	0/32	10/50	20/68	30/86	40/104
Surface Temp	-10/14	0/32	10/50	20/68	30/86	40/104
Temp @ Depth	-10/14	0/32	10/50	20/68	30/86	40/104
Surface	Calm		Choppy		Waves
Current	None				Swift
Visibility M/ft	0	7.5/25	15/50	23/75	30/100

Dive Profile

⬤ First Dive　⬤ Second Dive　⬤ Third Dive

D E P T H

Surface Interval	
Starting Group	
Time In		End Group
Pressure In		Safety Stop

Plan Depth	Maximum Depth	Bottom Time	Time Out	Pressure Out

TIME

Wetsuit	**Drysuit**	**Equipment**			
Full / Shorty	Liner	Weight _____ lb kg	⬤ Camera	⬤ Knife	⬤ Sausage
_____ mm	Argon	Tank _____ cuft L	⬤ Lighting	⬤ Flashlight	⬤ Float N Flag
		Pony tank _____ cuft L	⬤ Wreck reel	⬤ Spear gun	⬤ Lift bag
			⬤ Compass	⬤ Whistle	⬤ Float marker

Nitrox _____ %
(for air use 21%)

MOD _____ ft

Tri-Mix

O2 _____ % N _____ %

HE _____ %

Rebreather Scrubber Monitor

Dive Scrubber _____ Minutes

Total Scrubber _____ Minutes

Dive partner: _____ PADI NAUI ACUC Other

Email/phone: _____ Cert. Number: _____

Sightings, Hazards, Notes, Photos, Sketches

DIVER'S LOG BOOK

Dive Number:	Date:

Location:
GPS:
Body of Water:
Site:

Dive Class

- Wreck
- Shore
- Reef
- River
- Ice
- Deep
- Cave
- Boat
- Certify
- Photo
- Video
- _____
- _____
- _____

Weather	🌙	❄️	🌧️	⛅	☀️
Air Temp C/F	-10/14	0/32	10/50	20/68	30/86	40/104
Surface Temp	-10/14	0/32	10/50	20/68	30/86	40/104
Temp @ Depth	-10/14	0/32	10/50	20/68	30/86	40/104
Surface	Calm		Choppy		Waves
Current	None				Swift
Visibility M/ft	0	7.5/25	15/50	23/75	30/100

Dive Profile   ● First Dive   ● Second Dive   ● Third Dive

D E P T H

Surface Interval	
Starting Group	
Time In	End Group
Pressure In	Safety Stop

Plan Depth	Maximum Depth	Bottom Time	Time Out	Pressure Out

TIME

Wetsuit	**Drysuit**	**Equipment**		
Full / Shorty	Liner	Weight _____ lb kg	● Camera	● Knife	● Sausage
_____ mm	Argon	Tank _____ cuft L	● Lighting	● Flashlight	● Float N Flag
		Pony tank _____ cuft L	● Wreck reel	● Spear gun	● Lift bag
			● Compass	● Whistle	● Float marker

Nitrox _____% (for air use 21%) MOD_____ft	**Tri-Mix** O2 ____% N _____% HE ____%	**Rebreather Scrubber Monitor** Dive Scrubber_____ Minutes Total Scrubber _____ Minutes

Dive partner:_____ PADI NAUI ACUC Other

Email/phone:_____ Cert. Number: _____

Sightings, Hazards, Notes, Photos, Sketches

Dive Number:	Date:
Location:	
GPS:	
Body of Water:	
Site:	

Dive Class

- Wreck
- Shore
- Reef
- River
- Ice
- Deep
- Cave
- Boat
- Certify
- Photo
- Video
- _____
- _____
- _____

Weather	☾	❄	🌧	⛅	☀
Air Temp C/F	-10/14	0/32	10/50	20/68	30/86	40/104
Surface Temp	-10/14	0/32	10/50	20/68	30/86	40/104
Temp @ Depth	-10/14	0/32	10/50	20/68	30/86	40/104
Surface	Calm		Choppy		Waves
Current	None				Swift
Visibility M/ft	0	7.5/25	15/50	23/75	30/100

Dive Profile

- First Dive
- Second Dive
- Third Dive

DEPTH

Surface Interval				
Starting Group				
Time In			End Group	
Pressure In			Safety Stop	
Plan Depth	Maximum Depth	Bottom Time	Time Out	Pressure Out

TIME

Wetsuit	**Drysuit**
Full / Shorty	Liner
_____ mm	Argon

Equipment

Weight _____ lb kg
Tank _____ cuft L
Pony tank _____ cuft L

- Camera
- Lighting
- Wreck reel
- Compass
- Knife
- Flashlight
- Spear gun
- Whistle
- Sausage
- Float N Flag
- Lift bag
- Float marker

Nitrox _____ %
(for air use 21%)

MOD _____ ft

Tri-Mix

O2 _____ % N _____ %

HE _____ %

Rebreather Scrubber Monitor

Dive Scrubber _____ Minutes

Total Scrubber _____ Minutes

Dive partner: _____ PADI NAUI ACUC Other

Email/phone: _____ Cert. Number: _____

Sightings, Hazards, Notes, Photos, Sketches

DIVER'S LOG BOOK

Dive Number:		Date:	
Location:			
GPS:			
Body of Water:			
Site:			

Dive Class

- Wreck
- Shore
- Reef
- River
- Ice
- Deep
- Cave
- Boat
- Certify
- Photo
- Video
- _____
- _____
- _____

Weather	☾	❄	🌧	⛅	☀
Air Temp C/F	-10/14	0/32	10/50	20/68	30/86	40/104
Surface Temp	-10/14	0/32	10/50	20/68	30/86	40/104
Temp @ Depth	-10/14	0/32	10/50	20/68	30/86	40/104
Surface	Calm		Choppy		Waves
Current	None				Swift
Visibility M/ft	0	7.5/25	15/50	23/75	30/100

Dive Profile

- First Dive
- Second Dive
- Third Dive

DEPTH

Surface Interval	
Starting Group	
Time In	End Group
Pressure In	Safety Stop

Plan Depth	Maximum Depth	Bottom Time	Time Out	Pressure Out

TIME

Wetsuit — Full / Shorty — _____ mm

Drysuit — Liner — Argon

Equipment

Weight _____ lb kg
Tank _____ cuft L
Pony tank _____ cuft L

- Camera
- Lighting
- Wreck reel
- Compass
- Knife
- Flashlight
- Spear gun
- Whistle
- Sausage
- Float N Flag
- Lift bag
- Float marker

Nitrox _____ %
(for air use 21%)

MOD_____ ft

Tri-Mix

O2 _____ % N _____ %

HE _____ %

Rebreather Scrubber Monitor

Dive Scrubber_____ Minutes

Total Scrubber_____ Minutes

Dive partner:_____ PADI NAUI ACUC Other

Email/phone:_____ Cert. Number: _____

Sightings, Hazards, Notes, Photos, Sketches

Dive Number:		Date:
Location:		
GPS:		
Body of Water:		
Site:		

Dive Class

- ⬤ Wreck
- ⬤ Shore
- ⬤ Reef
- ⬤ River
- ⬤ Ice
- ⬤ Deep
- ⬤ Cave

- ⬤ Boat
- ⬤ Certify
- ⬤ Photo
- ⬤ Video
- ⬤ _____
- ⬤ _____
- ⬤ _____

Weather	☾	☁❄	☁☂	☀☁	☀
Air Temp C/F	-10/14	0/32	10/50	20/68	30/86	40/104
Surface Temp	-10/14	0/32	10/50	20/68	30/86	40/104
Temp @ Depth	-10/14	0/32	10/50	20/68	30/86	40/104
Surface	Calm		Choppy		Waves
Current	None				Swift
Visibility M/ft	0	7.5/25	15/50	23/75	30/100

Dive Profile

⬤ First Dive   ⬤ Second Dive   ⬤ Third Dive

DEPTH

Surface Interval				
Starting Group				
Time In				End Group
Pressure In				Safety Stop
Plan Depth	Maximum Depth	Bottom Time	Time Out	Pressure Out

TIME

Wetsuit   **Drysuit**
Full / Shorty   Liner
_____ mm   Argon

Equipment
Weight _____ lb kg
Tank _____ cuft L
Pony tank _____ cuft L

- ⬤ Camera
- ⬤ Lighting
- ⬤ Wreck reel
- ⬤ Compass

- ⬤ Knife
- ⬤ Flashlight
- ⬤ Spear gun
- ⬤ Whistle

- ⬤ Sausage
- ⬤ Float N Flag
- ⬤ Lift bag
- ⬤ Float marker

Nitrox _____ %
(for air use 21%)

MOD _____ ft

Tri-Mix
O2 ____ %   N ____ %
HE ____ %

Rebreather Scrubber Monitor
Dive Scrubber _____ Minutes
Total Scrubber _____ Minutes

Dive partner: _____ PADI   NAUI   ACUC   Other

Email/phone: _____ Cert. Number: _____

Sightings, Hazards, Notes, Photos, Sketches

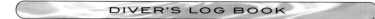

Dive Number:	Date:
Location:	
GPS:	
Body of Water:	
Site:	

Dive Class

- Wreck
- Shore
- Reef
- River
- Ice
- Deep
- Cave
- Boat
- Certify
- Photo
- Video
- _____
- _____
- _____

Weather	☾	❄	🌧	☁	☀
Air Temp C/F	-10/14	0/32	10/50	20/68	30/86	40/104
Surface Temp	-10/14	0/32	10/50	20/68	30/86	40/104
Temp @ Depth	-10/14	0/32	10/50	20/68	30/86	40/104
Surface	Calm		Choppy		Waves
Current	None				Swift
Visibility M/ft	0	7.5/25	15/50	23/75	30/100

Dive Profile

- First Dive
- Second Dive
- Third Dive

DEPTH

Surface Interval	
Starting Group	
Time In	End Group
Pressure In	Safety Stop

Plan Depth	Maximum Depth	Bottom Time	Time Out	Pressure Out

TIME

Wetsuit
Full / Shorty
_____ mm

Drysuit
Liner
Argon

Equipment
Weight _____ lb kg
Tank _____ cuft L
Pony tank _____ cuft L

- Camera
- Lighting
- Wreck reel
- Compass
- Knife
- Flashlight
- Spear gun
- Whistle
- Sausage
- Float N Flag
- Lift bag
- Float marker

Nitrox _____%
(for air use 21%)

MOD_____ft

Tri-Mix
O2 _____% N _____%
HE _____%

Rebreather Scrubber Monitor
Dive Scrubber_____ Minutes
Total Scrubber _____ Minutes

Dive partner:_____ PADI NAUI ACUC Other

Email/phone:_____ Cert. Number: _____

Sightings, Hazards, Notes, Photos, Sketches

DIVER'S LOG BOOK

	Dive Number:	Date:
	Location:	
	GPS:	
	Body of Water:	
	Site:	

Dive Class

- Wreck
- Shore
- Reef
- River
- Ice
- Deep
- Cave
- Boat
- Certify
- Photo
- Video
- _____
- _____
- _____

Weather	☾	☁❄	☁🌧	⛅	☀
Air Temp C/F	-10/14	0/32	10/50	20/68	30/86	40/104
Surface Temp	-10/14	0/32	10/50	20/68	30/86	40/104
Temp @ Depth	-10/14	0/32	10/50	20/68	30/86	40/104
Surface	Calm		Choppy		Waves
Current	None				Swift
Visibility M/ft	0	7.5/25	15/50	23/75	30/100

Dive Profile

● First Dive   ● Second Dive   ● Third Dive

D E P T H	Surface Interval		
	Starting Group		
	Time In		End Group
	Pressure In		Safety Stop
	Plan Depth	Maximum Depth	Bottom Time	Time Out	Pressure Out

TIME

Wetsuit	**Drysuit**	**Equipment**
Full / Shorty	Liner	Weight _____ lb kg
_____ mm	Argon	Tank _____ cuft L
		Pony tank _____ cuft L

- Camera
- Lighting
- Wreck reel
- Compass
- Knife
- Flashlight
- Spear gun
- Whistle
- Sausage
- Float N Flag
- Lift bag
- Float marker

Nitrox _____ %
(for air use 21%)

MOD _____ ft

Tri-Mix

O2 ____ %   N ____ %

HE ____ %

Rebreather Scrubber Monitor

Dive Scrubber _____ Minutes

Total Scrubber _____ Minutes

Dive partner: _____ PADI NAUI ACUC Other

Email/phone: _____ Cert. Number: _____

Sightings, Hazards, Notes, Photos, Sketches

Dive Number:	Date:
Location:	
GPS:	
Body of Water:	
Site:	

Dive Class

- Wreck
- Shore
- Reef
- River
- Ice
- Deep
- Cave
- Boat
- Certify
- Photo
- Video
- _____
- _____
- _____

Weather	☽	❄	🌧	⛅	☀
Air Temp C/F	-10/14	0/32	10/50	20/68	30/86	40/104
Surface Temp	-10/14	0/32	10/50	20/68	30/86	40/104
Temp @ Depth	-10/14	0/32	10/50	20/68	30/86	40/104
Surface	Calm		Choppy		Waves
Current	None				Swift
Visibility M/ft	0	7.5/25	15/50	23/75	30/100

Dive Profile

○ First Dive ○ Second Dive ○ Third Dive

DEPTH

Surface Interval	
Starting Group	
Time In	End Group
Pressure In	Safety Stop

Plan Depth	Maximum Depth	Bottom Time	Time Out	Pressure Out

TIME

Wetsuit   **Drysuit**

Full / Shorty   Liner

_____ mm   Argon

Equipment

Weight _____ lb kg

Tank _____ cuft L

Pony tank _____ cuft L

- Camera
- Lighting
- Wreck reel
- Compass
- Knife
- Flashlight
- Spear gun
- Whistle
- Sausage
- Float N Flag
- Lift bag
- Float marker

Nitrox _____%
(for air use 21%)

MOD _____ft

Tri-Mix

O2 _____% N _____%

HE _____%

Rebreather Scrubber Monitor

Dive Scrubber _____ Minutes

Total Scrubber _____ Minutes

Dive partner: _____ PADI   NAUI   ACUC   Other

Email/phone: _____ Cert. Number: _____

Sightings, Hazards, Notes, Photos, Sketches

DIVER'S LOG BOOK

Dive Number:	Date:

Location:
GPS:
Body of Water:
Site:

Dive Class

- Wreck
- Boat
- Shore
- Certify
- Reef
- Photo
- River
- Video
- Ice
- _____
- Deep
- _____
- Cave
- _____

Weather	☾	☁❄	🌧	⛅	☀
Air Temp C/F	-10/14	0/32	10/50	20/68	30/86	40/104
Surface Temp	-10/14	0/32	10/50	20/68	30/86	40/104
Temp @ Depth	-10/14	0/32	10/50	20/68	30/86	40/104
Surface	Calm		Choppy		Waves
Current	None				Swift
Visibility M/ft	0	7.5/25	15/50	23/75	30/100

Dive Profile

- First Dive
- Second Dive
- Third Dive

DEPTH

Surface Interval	
Starting Group	
Time In	End Group
Pressure In	Safety Stop

Plan Depth	Maximum Depth	Bottom Time	Time Out	Pressure Out

TIME

Wetsuit	**Drysuit**	**Equipment**
Full / Shorty	Liner	Weight _____ lb kg
_____ mm	Argon	Tank _____ cuft L
		Pony tank _____ cuft L

- Camera
- Knife
- Sausage
- Lighting
- Flashlight
- Float N Flag
- Wreck reel
- Spear gun
- Lift bag
- Compass
- Whistle
- Float marker

Nitrox _____% (for air use 21%)	**Tri-Mix**	**Rebreather Scrubber Monitor**
MOD_____ft	O2 ____% N ____%	Dive Scrubber _____ Minutes
	HE ____%	Total Scrubber _____ Minutes

Dive partner:_____ PADI NAUI ACUC Other

Email/phone:_____ Cert. Number: _____

Sightings, Hazards, Notes, Photos, Sketches

Dive Number:		Date:
Location:		
GPS:		
Body of Water:		
Site:		

Dive Class

- Wreck
- Shore
- Reef
- River
- Ice
- Deep
- Cave
- Boat
- Certify
- Photo
- Video
- _____
- _____
- _____

Weather	☾	❄☁	🌧☁	☁☀	☀
Air Temp C/F	-10/14	0/32	10/50	20/68	30/86	40/104
Surface Temp	-10/14	0/32	10/50	20/68	30/86	40/104
Temp @ Depth	-10/14	0/32	10/50	20/68	30/86	40/104
Surface	Calm		Choppy		Waves
Current	None				Swift
Visibility M/ft	0	7.5/25	15/50	23/75	30/100

Dive Profile

○ First Dive ○ Second Dive ○ Third Dive

DEPTH

Surface Interval	
Starting Group	
Time In	End Group
Pressure In	Safety Stop

Plan Depth	Maximum Depth	Bottom Time	Time Out	Pressure Out

TIME

Wetsuit
Full / Shorty
_____ mm

Drysuit
Liner
Argon

Equipment
Weight _____ lb kg
Tank _____ cuft L
Pony tank _____ cuft L

- Camera
- Lighting
- Wreck reel
- Compass
- Knife
- Flashlight
- Spear gun
- Whistle
- Sausage
- Float N Flag
- Lift bag
- Float marker

Nitrox _____ %
(for air use 21%)

MOD _____ ft

Tri-Mix
O2 _____ % N _____ %
HE _____ %

Rebreather Scrubber Monitor
Dive Scrubber _____ Minutes
Total Scrubber _____ Minutes

Dive partner: _____ PADI NAUI ACUC Other

Email/phone: _____ Cert. Number: _____

Sightings, Hazards, Notes, Photos, Sketches

Dive Number:		Date:
Location:		
GPS:		
Body of Water:		
Site:		

Dive Class

- Wreck
- Shore
- Reef
- River
- Ice
- Deep
- Cave
- Boat
- Certify
- Photo
- Video
- _____
- _____
- _____

Weather	🌙	❄️	🌧️	⛅	☀️
Air Temp C/F	-10/14	0/32	10/50	20/68	30/86	40/104
Surface Temp	-10/14	0/32	10/50	20/68	30/86	40/104
Temp @ Depth	-10/14	0/32	10/50	20/68	30/86	40/104
Surface	Calm		Choppy		Waves
Current	None				Swift
Visibility M/ft	0	7.5/25	15/50	23/75	30/100

Dive Profile

- First Dive
- Second Dive
- Third Dive

DEPTH

Surface Interval	
Starting Group	
Time In	End Group
Pressure In	Safety Stop

Plan Depth	Maximum Depth	Bottom Time	Time Out	Pressure Out

TIME

Wetsuit	**Drysuit**	**Equipment**	
Full / Shorty	Liner	Weight _____ lb kg	
_____ mm	Argon	Tank _____ cuft L	
		Pony tank ____ cuft L	

- Camera
- Lighting
- Wreck reel
- Compass
- Knife
- Flashlight
- Spear gun
- Whistle
- Sausage
- Float N Flag
- Lift bag
- Float marker

Nitrox _____ % (for air use 21%) MOD_____ ft	**Tri-Mix** O2 ____ % N ____ % HE ____ %	**Rebreather Scrubber Monitor** Dive Scrubber_____ Minutes Total Scrubber _____ Minutes

Dive partner: _____ PADI NAUI ACUC Other

Email/phone: _____ Cert. Number: _____

Sightings, Hazards, Notes, Photos, Sketches

DIVER'S LOG BOOK

Dive Number:		Date:
Location:		
GPS:		
Body of Water:		
Site:		

Dive Class

- Wreck
- Boat
- Shore
- Certify
- Reef
- Photo
- River
- Video
- Ice
- _____
- Deep
- _____
- Cave
- _____

Weather	☾	❄	☔	⛅	☀
Air Temp C/F	-10/14	0/32	10/50	20/68	30/86	40/104
Surface Temp	-10/14	0/32	10/50	20/68	30/86	40/104
Temp @ Depth	-10/14	0/32	10/50	20/68	30/86	40/104
Surface	Calm		Choppy		Waves
Current	None				Swift
Visibility M/ft	0	7.5/25	15/50	23/75	30/100

Dive Profile

- First Dive
- Second Dive
- Third Dive

DEPTH

Surface Interval			
Starting Group			
Time In			End Group
Pressure In			Safety Stop
Plan Depth	Maximum Depth	Bottom Time	Time Out	Pressure Out

TIME

Wetsuit	**Drysuit**	**Equipment**	
Full / Shorty	Liner	Weight _____ lb kg	
_____ mm	Argon	Tank _____ cuft L	
		Pony tank _____ cuft L	

- Camera
- Knife
- Sausage
- Lighting
- Flashlight
- Float N Flag
- Wreck reel
- Spear gun
- Lift bag
- Compass
- Whistle
- Float marker

Nitrox _____% (for air use 21%)	**Tri-Mix**	**Rebreather Scrubber Monitor**
MOD_____ft	O2 ____% N ____% HE ____%	Dive Scrubber _____ Minutes
		Total Scrubber _____ Minutes

Dive partner: _____ PADI NAUI ACUC Other

Email/phone: _____ Cert. Number: _____

Sightings, Hazards, Notes, Photos, Sketches

Dive Number:	Date:
Location:	
GPS:	
Body of Water:	
Site:	

Dive Class

- Wreck
- Boat
- Shore
- Certify
- Reef
- Photo
- River
- Video
- Ice
- ____
- Deep
- ____
- Cave
- ____

Weather	☾	❄	🌧	☁	☀
Air Temp C/F	-10/14	0/32	10/50	20/68	30/86	40/104
Surface Temp	-10/14	0/32	10/50	20/68	30/86	40/104
Temp @ Depth	-10/14	0/32	10/50	20/68	30/86	40/104
Surface	Calm		Choppy		Waves
Current	None				Swift
Visibility M/ft	0	7.5/25	15/50	23/75	30/100

Dive Profile

- First Dive
- Second Dive
- Third Dive

DEPTH

Surface Interval		
Starting Group		
Time In		End Group
Pressure In		Safety Stop
Plan Depth	Maximum Depth	Bottom Time	Time Out	Pressure Out

TIME

Wetsuit	**Drysuit**
Full / Shorty	Liner
____ mm	Argon

Equipment

Weight _____ lb kg
Tank _____ cuft L
Pony tank _____ cuft L

- Camera
- Knife
- Sausage
- Lighting
- Flashlight
- Float N Flag
- Wreck reel
- Spear gun
- Lift bag
- Compass
- Whistle
- Float marker

Nitrox _____%
(for air use 21%)

MOD_____ft

Tri-Mix

O2 ____% N ____%
HE ____%

Rebreather Scrubber Monitor

Dive Scrubber_____ Minutes
Total Scrubber_____ Minutes

Dive partner:_____ PADI NAUI ACUC Other

Email/phone:_____ Cert. Number: _____

Sightings, Hazards, Notes, Photos, Sketches

DIVER'S LOG BOOK

Dive Number:	Date:

| Location: |
| GPS: |
| Body of Water: |
| Site: |

Dive Class

● Wreck	● Boat
● Shore	● Certify
● Reef	● Photo
● River	● Video
● Ice	● _____
● Deep	● _____
● Cave	● _____

Weather	☾	❄	🌧	⛅	☀
Air Temp C/F	-10/14	0/32	10/50	20/68	30/86	40/104
Surface Temp	-10/14	0/32	10/50	20/68	30/86	40/104
Temp @ Depth	-10/14	0/32	10/50	20/68	30/86	40/104
Surface	Calm		Choppy		Waves
Current	None				Swift
Visibility M/ft	0	7.5/25	15/50	23/75	30/100

Dive Profile

● First Dive ● Second Dive ● Third Dive

DEPTH

Surface Interval	
Starting Group	
Time In	End Group
Pressure In	Safety Stop

Plan Depth	Maximum Depth	Bottom Time	Time Out	Pressure Out

TIME

Wetsuit	**Drysuit**
Full / Shorty	Liner
_____ mm	Argon

Equipment
Weight _____ lb kg
Tank _____ cuft L
Pony tank _____ cuft L

● Camera	● Knife	● Sausage
● Lighting	● Flashlight	● Float N Flag
● Wreck reel	● Spear gun	● Lift bag
● Compass	● Whistle	● Float marker

Nitrox _____%
(for air use 21%)

MOD_____ft

Tri-Mix
O2 ____% N ____%
HE ____%

Rebreather Scrubber Monitor
Dive Scrubber_____ Minutes
Total Scrubber_____ Minutes

Dive partner:_____ PADI NAUI ACUC Other

Email/phone:_____ Cert. Number: _____

Sightings, Hazards, Notes, Photos, Sketches

Dive Number:	Date:
Location:	
GPS:	
Body of Water:	
Site:	

Dive Class

- ◯ Wreck
- ◯ Boat
- ◯ Shore
- ◯ Certify
- ◯ Reef
- ◯ Photo
- ◯ River
- ◯ Video
- ◯ Ice
- ◯ _____
- ◯ Deep
- ◯ _____
- ◯ Cave
- ◯ _____

Weather	🌙	❄️	🌧️	☁️	☀️
Air Temp C/F	-10/14	0/32	10/50	20/68	30/86	40/104
Surface Temp	-10/14	0/32	10/50	20/68	30/86	40/104
Temp @ Depth	-10/14	0/32	10/50	20/68	30/86	40/104
Surface	Calm		Choppy		Waves
Current	None				Swift
Visibility M/ft	0	7.5/25	15/50	23/75	30/100

Dive Profile

◯ First Dive ◯ Second Dive ◯ Third Dive

DEPTH

Surface Interval		
Starting Group		
Time In		End Group
Pressure In		Safety Stop
Plan Depth	Maximum Depth	Bottom Time	Time Out	Pressure Out

TIME

Wetsuit **Drysuit**

Full / Shorty   Liner

_____ mm   Argon

Equipment

Weight _____ lb kg
Tank _____ cuft L
Pony tank _____ cuft L

- ◯ Camera
- ◯ Knife
- ◯ Sausage
- ◯ Lighting
- ◯ Flashlight
- ◯ Float N Flag
- ◯ Wreck reel
- ◯ Spear gun
- ◯ Lift bag
- ◯ Compass
- ◯ Whistle
- ◯ Float marker

Nitrox _____%
(for air use 21%)

MOD _____ ft

Tri-Mix

O2 _____% N _____%
HE _____%

Rebreather Scrubber Monitor

Dive Scrubber _____ Minutes
Total Scrubber _____ Minutes

Dive partner: _____ PADI NAUI ACUC Other

Email/phone: _____ Cert. Number: _____

Sightings, Hazards, Notes, Photos, Sketches

Dive Number:	Date:
Location:	
GPS:	
Body of Water:	
Site:	

Dive Class

- Wreck
- Shore
- Reef
- River
- Ice
- Deep
- Cave
- Boat
- Certify
- Photo
- Video
- _____
- _____
- _____

Weather	🌙	❄	🌧	⛅	☀
Air Temp C/F	-10/14	0/32	10/50	20/68	30/86	40/104
Surface Temp	-10/14	0/32	10/50	20/68	30/86	40/104
Temp @ Depth	-10/14	0/32	10/50	20/68	30/86	40/104
Surface	Calm		Choppy		Waves
Current	None				Swift
Visibility M/ft	0	7.5/25	15/50	23/75	30/100

Dive Profile

First Dive   Second Dive   Third Dive

Surface Interval				
Starting Group				
Time In			End Group	
Pressure In			Safety Stop	
Plan Depth	Maximum Depth	Bottom Time	Time Out	Pressure Out

DEPTH

TIME

Wetsuit	**Drysuit**	**Equipment**			
Full / Shorty	Liner	Weight _____ lb kg	Camera	Knife	Sausage
_____ mm	Argon	Tank _____ cuft L	Lighting	Flashlight	Float N Flag
		Pony tank _____ cuft L	Wreck reel	Spear gun	Lift bag
			Compass	Whistle	Float marker

Nitrox _____% (for air use 21%)	**Tri-Mix**	**Rebreather Scrubber Monitor**
MOD _____ ft	O2 ____% N ____% HE ____%	Dive Scrubber _____ Minutes Total Scrubber _____ Minutes

Dive partner: _____ PADI NAUI ACUC Other

Email/phone: _____ Cert. Number: _____

Sightings, Hazards, Notes, Photos, Sketches

DIVER'S LOG BOOK

Dive Number:		Date:
Location:		
GPS:		
Body of Water:		
Site:		

Dive Class

○ Wreck	○ Boat
○ Shore	○ Certify
○ Reef	○ Photo
○ River	○ Video
○ Ice	○ _____
○ Deep	○ _____
○ Cave	○ _____

Weather	☾	☁❄	🌧	⛅	☀
Air Temp C/F	-10/14	0/32	10/50	20/68	30/86	40/104
Surface Temp	-10/14	0/32	10/50	20/68	30/86	40/104
Temp @ Depth	-10/14	0/32	10/50	20/68	30/86	40/104
Surface	Calm		Choppy		Waves
Current	None				Swift
Visibility M/ft	0	7.5/25	15/50	23/75	30/100

Dive Profile

○ First Dive ○ Second Dive ○ Third Dive

DEPTH

Surface Interval	
Starting Group	
Time In	End Group
Pressure In	Safety Stop

Plan Depth	Maximum Depth	Bottom Time	Time Out	Pressure Out

TIME

Wetsuit	**Drysuit**	**Equipment**		
Full / Shorty	Liner	Weight _____ lb kg	○ Camera	○ Knife	○ Sausage
_____ mm	Argon	Tank _____ cuft L	○ Lighting	○ Flashlight	○ Float N Flag
		Pony tank _____ cuft L	○ Wreck reel	○ Spear gun	○ Lift bag
			○ Compass	○ Whistle	○ Float marker

Nitrox _____ % (for air use 21%)	**Tri-Mix**	**Rebreather Scrubber Monitor**
MOD _____ ft	O2 ____ % N ____ % HE ____ %	Dive Scrubber _____ Minutes Total Scrubber _____ Minutes

Dive partner: _____ PADI NAUI ACUC Other

Email/phone: _____ Cert. Number: _____

Sightings, Hazards, Notes, Photos, Sketches

DIVER'S LOG BOOK

Dive Number:	Date:
Location:	
GPS:	
Body of Water:	
Site:	

Dive Class

- Wreck
- Shore
- Reef
- River
- Ice
- Deep
- Cave
- Boat
- Certify
- Photo
- Video
- _____
- _____
- _____

Weather	$\,$	$\,$	$\,$	$\,$	$\,$	$\,$
Air Temp C/F	-10/14	0/32	10/50	20/68	30/86	40/104
Surface Temp	-10/14	0/32	10/50	20/68	30/86	40/104
Temp @ Depth	-10/14	0/32	10/50	20/68	30/86	40/104
Surface	Calm		Choppy			Waves
Current	None					Swift
Visibility M/ft	0	7.5/25	15/50		23/75	30/100

Dive Profile

- First Dive
- Second Dive
- Third Dive

DEPTH

Surface Interval	
Starting Group	
Time In	End Group
Pressure In	Safety Stop
Plan Depth	Maximum Depth	Bottom Time	Time Out	Pressure Out

TIME

Wetsuit	**Drysuit**	**Equipment**
Full / Shorty	Liner	Weight _____ lb kg
_____ mm	Argon	Tank _____ cuft L
		Pony tank _____ cuft L

- Camera
- Lighting
- Wreck reel
- Compass
- Knife
- Flashlight
- Spear gun
- Whistle
- Sausage
- Float N Flag
- Lift bag
- Float marker

Nitrox _____ %
(for air use 21%)

MOD _____ ft

Tri-Mix

O2 _____ % N _____ %

HE _____ %

Rebreather Scrubber Monitor

Dive Scrubber _____ Minutes

Total Scrubber _____ Minutes

Dive partner: _____ PADI NAUI ACUC Other

Email/phone: _____ Cert. Number: _____

Sightings, Hazards, Notes, Photos, Sketches

DIVER'S LOG BOOK

Dive Number:	Date:

Location:
GPS:
Body of Water:
Site:

Dive Class

⦾ Wreck	⦾ Boat
⦾ Shore	⦾ Certify
⦾ Reef	⦾ Photo
⦾ River	⦾ Video
⦾ Ice	⦾ _____
⦾ Deep	⦾ _____
⦾ Cave	⦾ _____

Weather	🌙	❄️	🌧️	⛅	☀️
Air Temp C/F	-10/14	0/32	10/50	20/68	30/86	40/104
Surface Temp	-10/14	0/32	10/50	20/68	30/86	40/104
Temp @ Depth	-10/14	0/32	10/50	20/68	30/86	40/104
Surface	Calm		Choppy		Waves
Current	None				Swift
Visibility M/ft	0	7.5/25	15/50	23/75	30/100

Dive Profile

⦾ First Dive　⦾ Second Dive　⦾ Third Dive

D E P T H	Surface Interval	
	Starting Group	
	Time In	End Group
	Pressure In	Safety Stop
	Plan Depth	Maximum Depth	Bottom Time	Time Out	Pressure Out

TIME

Wetsuit	Drysuit
Full / Shorty	Liner
_____ mm	Argon

Equipment

Weight _____ lb kg
Tank _____ cuft L
Pony tank _____ cuft L

⦾ Camera	⦾ Knife	⦾ Sausage
⦾ Lighting	⦾ Flashlight	⦾ Float N Flag
⦾ Wreck reel	⦾ Spear gun	⦾ Lift bag
⦾ Compass	⦾ Whistle	⦾ Float marker

Nitrox _____%
(for air use 21%)

MOD_____ft

Tri-Mix

O2 ____% N ____%
HE ____%

Rebreather Scrubber Monitor

Dive Scrubber_____ Minutes
Total Scrubber_____ Minutes

Dive partner:_____ PADI NAUI ACUC Other

Email/phone:_____ Cert. Number: _____

Sightings, Hazards, Notes, Photos, Sketches

DIVER'S LOG BOOK

Dive Number:		Date:	
Location:			
GPS:			
Body of Water:			
Site:			

Dive Class

- Wreck
- Shore
- Reef
- River
- Ice
- Deep
- Cave
- Boat
- Certify
- Photo
- Video
- _____
- _____
- _____

Weather	☽	❄❄	🌧	⛅	☀
Air Temp C/F	-10/14	0/32	10/50	20/68	30/86	40/104
Surface Temp	-10/14	0/32	10/50	20/68	30/86	40/104
Temp @ Depth	-10/14	0/32	10/50	20/68	30/86	40/104
Surface	Calm		Choppy		Waves
Current	None				Swift
Visibility M/ft	0	7.5/25	15/50	23/75	30/100

Dive Profile

- First Dive
- Second Dive
- Third Dive

DEPTH

Surface Interval	
Starting Group	
Time In	End Group
Pressure In	Safety Stop

Plan Depth	Maximum Depth	Bottom Time	Time Out	Pressure Out

TIME

Wetsuit	**Drysuit**	**Equipment**	
Full / Shorty	Liner	Weight _____ lb kg	
_____ mm	Argon	Tank _____ cuft L	
		Pony tank _____ cuft L	

- Camera
- Lighting
- Wreck reel
- Compass
- Knife
- Flashlight
- Spear gun
- Whistle
- Sausage
- Float N Flag
- Lift bag
- Float marker

Nitrox _____ % (for air use 21%)	**Tri-Mix**	**Rebreather Scrubber Monitor**
MOD _____ ft	O2 ____% N ____%	Dive Scrubber _____ Minutes
	HE ____%	Total Scrubber _____ Minutes

Dive partner: _____ PADI NAUI ACUC Other

Email/phone: _____ Cert. Number: _____

Sightings, Hazards, Notes, Photos, Sketches

	Dive Number:	Date:
	Location:	
	GPS:	
	Body of Water:	
	Site:	

Dive Class

- ○ Wreck
- ○ Boat
- ○ Shore
- ○ Certify
- ○ Reef
- ○ Photo
- ○ River
- ○ Video
- ○ Ice
- ○ _____
- ○ Deep
- ○ _____
- ○ Cave
- ○ _____

Weather	☾	☁❄	🌧	⛅	☀
Air Temp C/F	-10/14	0/32	10/50	20/68	30/86	40/104
Surface Temp	-10/14	0/32	10/50	20/68	30/86	40/104
Temp @ Depth	-10/14	0/32	10/50	20/68	30/86	40/104
Surface	Calm		Choppy		Waves
Current	None				Swift
Visibility M/ft	0	7.5/25	15/50	23/75	30/100

Dive Profile   ○ First Dive   ○ Second Dive   ○ Third Dive

D E P T H	Surface Interval		
	Starting Group		
	Time In		End Group
	Pressure In		Safety Stop
	Plan Depth	Maximum Depth	Bottom Time	Time Out	Pressure Out

TIME

Wetsuit	**Drysuit**	**Equipment**		
Full / Shorty	Liner	Weight _____ lb kg	○ Camera	○ Knife	○ Sausage
____ mm	Argon	Tank _____ cuft L	○ Lighting	○ Flashlight	○ Float N Flag
		Pony tank ____ cuft L	○ Wreck reel	○ Spear gun	○ Lift bag
			○ Compass	○ Whistle	○ Float marker

Nitrox _____% (for air use 21%) MOD_____ft	**Tri-Mix** O2 ____% N ____% HE ____%	**Rebreather Scrubber Monitor** Dive Scrubber_____ Minutes Total Scrubber_____ Minutes

Dive partner:_____ PADI NAUI ACUC Other

Email/phone:_____ Cert. Number: _____

Sightings, Hazards, Notes, Photos, Sketches

DIVER'S LOG BOOK

Dive Number:	Date:
Location:	
GPS:	
Body of Water:	
Site:	

Dive Class

- ◉ Wreck
- ◉ Shore
- ◉ Reef
- ◉ River
- ◉ Ice
- ◉ Deep
- ◉ Cave
- ◉ Boat
- ◉ Certify
- ◉ Photo
- ◉ Video
- ◉ _____
- ◉ _____
- ◉ _____

Weather	☾	☁❅❅	☁⛆	☀☁	☀
Air Temp C/F	-10/14	0/32	10/50	20/68	30/86	40/104
Surface Temp	-10/14	0/32	10/50	20/68	30/86	40/104
Temp @ Depth	-10/14	0/32	10/50	20/68	30/86	40/104
Surface	Calm		Choppy		Waves
Current	None				Swift
Visibility M/ft	0	7.5/25	15/50	23/75	30/100

Dive Profile

◉ First Dive ◉ Second Dive ◉ Third Dive

DEPTH

Surface Interval	
Starting Group	
Time In	End Group
Pressure In	Safety Stop

Plan Depth	Maximum Depth	Bottom Time	Time Out	Pressure Out

TIME

Wetsuit	**Drysuit**	**Equipment**
Full / Shorty	Liner	Weight _____ lb kg
_____ mm	Argon	Tank _____ cuft L
		Pony tank _____ cuft L

- ◉ Camera
- ◉ Lighting
- ◉ Wreck reel
- ◉ Compass
- ◉ Knife
- ◉ Flashlight
- ◉ Spear gun
- ◉ Whistle
- ◉ Sausage
- ◉ Float N Flag
- ◉ Lift bag
- ◉ Float marker

Nitrox _____ %
(for air use 21%)

MOD _____ ft

Tri-Mix

O2 _____ % N _____ %

HE _____ %

Rebreather Scrubber Monitor

Dive Scrubber _____ Minutes

Total Scrubber _____ Minutes

Dive partner: _____ PADI NAUI ACUC Other

Email/phone: _____ Cert. Number: _____

Sightings, Hazards, Notes, Photos, Sketches

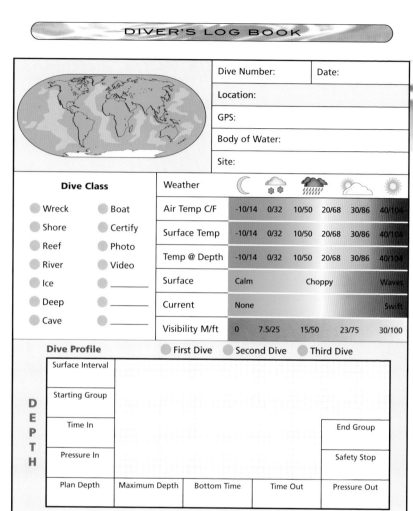

Dive Number:		Date:	
Location:			
GPS:			
Body of Water:			
Site:			

Dive Class

- ○ Wreck
- ○ Shore
- ○ Reef
- ○ River
- ○ Ice
- ○ Deep
- ○ Cave
- ○ Boat
- ○ Certify
- ○ Photo
- ○ Video
- ○ _____
- ○ _____
- ○ _____

Weather	☾	☁❄	☁🌧	⛅	☀
Air Temp C/F	-10/14	0/32	10/50	20/68	30/86	40/104
Surface Temp	-10/14	0/32	10/50	20/68	30/86	40/104
Temp @ Depth	-10/14	0/32	10/50	20/68	30/86	40/104
Surface	Calm		Choppy		Waves
Current	None				Swift
Visibility M/ft	0	7.5/25	15/50	23/75	30/100

Dive Profile

○ First Dive   ○ Second Dive   ○ Third Dive

DEPTH

Surface Interval				
Starting Group				
Time In				End Group
Pressure In				Safety Stop
Plan Depth	Maximum Depth	Bottom Time	Time Out	Pressure Out

TIME

Wetsuit	**Drysuit**	**Equipment**			
Full / Shorty	Liner	Weight _____ lb kg	○ Camera	○ Knife	○ Sausage
_____ mm	Argon	Tank _____ cuft L	○ Lighting	○ Flashlight	○ Float N Flag
		Pony tank _____ cuft L	○ Wreck reel	○ Spear gun	○ Lift bag
			○ Compass	○ Whistle	○ Float marker

Nitrox _____ % (for air use 21%) MOD _____ ft	**Tri-Mix** O2 _____ % N _____ % HE _____ %	**Rebreather Scrubber Monitor** Dive Scrubber _____ Minutes Total Scrubber _____ Minutes

Dive partner: _____ PADI NAUI ACUC Other

Email/phone: _____ Cert. Number: _____

Sightings, Hazards, Notes, Photos, Sketches

DIVER'S LOG BOOK

Dive Number:	Date:

| Location: |
| GPS: |
| Body of Water: |
| Site: |

Dive Class

- ○ Wreck
- ○ Boat
- ○ Shore
- ○ Certify
- ○ Reef
- ○ Photo
- ○ River
- ○ Video
- ○ Ice
- ○ _____
- ○ Deep
- ○ _____
- ○ Cave
- ○ _____

Weather	☾	❄	🌧	☁	☀
Air Temp C/F	-10/14	0/32	10/50	20/68	30/86	40/104
Surface Temp	-10/14	0/32	10/50	20/68	30/86	40/104
Temp @ Depth	-10/14	0/32	10/50	20/68	30/86	40/104
Surface	Calm		Choppy		Waves
Current	None				Swift
Visibility M/ft	0	7.5/25	15/50	23/75	30/100

Dive Profile   ○ First Dive   ○ Second Dive   ○ Third Dive

D E P T H

Surface Interval	
Starting Group	
Time In		End Group
Pressure In		Safety Stop

| Plan Depth | Maximum Depth | Bottom Time | Time Out | Pressure Out |

TIME

Wetsuit	**Drysuit**	**Equipment**
Full / Shorty	Liner	Weight _____ lb kg
_____ mm	Argon	Tank _____ cuft L
		Pony tank _____ cuft L

- ○ Camera
- ○ Knife
- ○ Sausage
- ○ Lighting
- ○ Flashlight
- ○ Float N Flag
- ○ Wreck reel
- ○ Spear gun
- ○ Lift bag
- ○ Compass
- ○ Whistle
- ○ Float marker

Nitrox _____ %
(for air use 21%)

MOD_____ ft

Tri-Mix

O2 _____ %   N _____ %

HE _____ %

Rebreather Scrubber Monitor

Dive Scrubber_____ Minutes

Total Scrubber_____ Minutes

Dive partner:_____ PADI NAUI ACUC Other

Email/phone:_____ Cert. Number: _____

Sightings, Hazards, Notes, Photos, Sketches

DIVER'S LOG BOOK

Dive Number:	Date:
Location:	
GPS:	
Body of Water:	
Site:	

Dive Class

- Wreck
- Shore
- Reef
- River
- Ice
- Deep
- Cave
- Boat
- Certify
- Photo
- Video
- _____
- _____
- _____

Weather	☾	☁❄	⛈	⛅	☀
Air Temp C/F	-10/14	0/32	10/50	20/68	30/86	40/104
Surface Temp	-10/14	0/32	10/50	20/68	30/86	40/104
Temp @ Depth	-10/14	0/32	10/50	20/68	30/86	40/104
Surface	Calm		Choppy		Waves
Current	None				Swift
Visibility M/ft	0	7.5/25	15/50	23/75	30/100

Dive Profile

- First Dive
- Second Dive
- Third Dive

DEPTH

Surface Interval	
Starting Group	
Time In	End Group
Pressure In	Safety Stop

Plan Depth	Maximum Depth	Bottom Time	Time Out	Pressure Out

TIME

Wetsuit
Full / Shorty
_____ mm

Drysuit
Liner
Argon

Equipment
Weight _____ lb kg
Tank _____ cuft L
Pony tank _____ cuft L

- Camera
- Lighting
- Wreck reel
- Compass
- Knife
- Flashlight
- Spear gun
- Whistle
- Sausage
- Float N Flag
- Lift bag
- Float marker

Nitrox _____ %
(for air use 21%)

MOD _____ ft

Tri-Mix
O2 ____ % N ____ %
HE ____ %

Rebreather Scrubber Monitor
Dive Scrubber _____ Minutes
Total Scrubber _____ Minutes

Dive partner: _____ PADI NAUI ACUC Other

Email/phone: _____ Cert. Number: _____

Sightings, Hazards, Notes, Photos, Sketches

Annual Recap of Diving

Year _____

Number of Dives _____

_____

Highlights _____

Annual Recap of Diving

Year _____

Number of Dives _____

_____

Highlights _____

Annual Recap of Diving

Year _____

Number of Dives _____

_____

Highlights _____

Annual Recap of Diving

Year _____

Number of Dives _____

_____

Highlights _____

Annual Recap of Diving

Year _____

Number of Dives _____

_____

Highlights _____

Annual Recap of Diving

Year _____

Number of Dives _____

_____

Highlights _____

Annual Recap of Diving

Year _____

Number of Dives _____

_____

Highlights _____

Annual Recap of Diving

Year _____

Number of Dives _____

_____

Highlights _____

Annual Recap of Diving

Year _____

Number of Dives _____

_____

Highlights _____

Annual Recap of Diving

Year _____

Number of Dives _____

_____

Highlights _____

Dive Buddies

Name _____

Address _____

_____

Home Tel. _____ Business Tel. _____

Cell _____ Email _____

Name _____

Address _____

_____

Home Tel. _____ Business Tel. _____

Cell _____ Email _____

Name _____

Address _____

_____

Home Tel. _____ Business Tel. _____

Cell _____ Email _____

Name _____

Address _____

_____

Home Tel. _____ Business Tel. _____

Cell _____ Email _____

Dive Buddies

Name _____

Address _____

_____

Home Tel. _____ Business Tel. _____

Cell _____ Email _____

Name _____

Address _____

_____

Home Tel. _____ Business Tel. _____

Cell _____ Email _____

Name _____

Address _____

_____

Home Tel. _____ Business Tel. _____

Cell _____ Email _____

Name _____

Address _____

_____

Home Tel. _____ Business Tel. _____

Cell _____ Email _____

Dive Buddies

Name _____

Address _____

_____

Home Tel. _____ Business Tel. _____

Cell _____ Email _____

Name _____

Address _____

_____

Home Tel. _____ Business Tel. _____

Cell _____ Email _____

Name _____

Address _____

_____

Home Tel. _____ Business Tel. _____

Cell _____ Email _____

Name _____

Address _____

_____

Home Tel. _____ Business Tel. _____

Cell _____ Email _____

Dive Buddies

Name _____

Address _____

_____

Home Tel. _____ Business Tel. _____

Cell _____ Email _____

Name _____

Address _____

_____

Home Tel. _____ Business Tel. _____

Cell _____ Email _____

Name _____

Address _____

_____

Home Tel. _____ Business Tel. _____

Cell _____ Email _____

Name _____

Address _____

_____

Home Tel. _____ Business Tel. _____

Cell _____ Email _____

Dive Buddies

Name _____

Address _____

_____

Home Tel. _____ Business Tel. _____

Cell _____ Email _____

Name _____

Address _____

_____

Home Tel. _____ Business Tel. _____

Cell _____ Email _____

Name _____

Address _____

_____

Home Tel. _____ Business Tel. _____

Cell _____ Email _____

Name _____

Address _____

_____

Home Tel. _____ Business Tel. _____

Cell _____ Email _____

Dive Buddies

Name _____

Address _____

_____

Home Tel. _____ Business Tel. _____

Cell _____ Email _____

Name _____

Address _____

_____

Home Tel. _____ Business Tel. _____

Cell _____ Email _____

Name _____

Address _____

_____

Home Tel. _____ Business Tel. _____

Cell _____ Email _____

Name _____

Address _____

_____

Home Tel. _____ Business Tel. _____

Cell _____ Email _____

Authors

Dean McConnachie has logged over 800 dives throughout North America and the Caribbean. He is a PADI nitrox-certified ACUC advanced diver, a qualified rescue scuba diver, and has filmed many shipwreck sites on the Great Lakes and along the east coast as part of the Get Wrecked dive team. He lives on the water in Port Credit, Ontario.

Christine Marks received ACUC Basic Diver certification through the Burlington (Ontario) Marlins Dive Club. Her previous book was *Interstate 75 and the 401*, a guide for "snowbirds" traveling between Ontario and Florida. She lives in Hamilton, Ontario.